WHAT I HAVE LIVED BY

an autobiography

Charles L. ALLEN

Fleming H. Revell Company

Old Tappan, New Jersey

Scripture references in this volume are from the King James Version of the Bible

"The Song of a Heathen" by Richard Gilder is from *Beautiful Poems on Jesus,* Basil Miller, compiler. © 1948, Beacon Hill Press, Kansas City, Missouri. Used by permission.

Excerpt from TOO TRUE TO BE GOOD by George Bernard Shaw is used by permission of The Society of Authors on behalf of the Bernard Shaw estate.

Library of Congress Cataloging in Publication Data

Allen, Charles Livingstone, date
    What I Have Lived By

    1. Allen, Charles Livingstone, date
2. Methodist Church—Clergy—Biography.   3. Clergy
BX8495.A518A33   287'.6'0924 [B]   76-40914
ISBN 0-8007-0805-9
ISBN 0-8007-0806-7 gift ed.

Contents

To the ones I love the most

Leila Jane Haynes Allen

Charles L. Allen, Jr.
Kay deMange Allen
    Charles L. Allen III
    Margaret Ann Allen
    Jack deMange Allen

Franklin Allen
Ann Woolsey Allen
    Franklin Allen, Jr.
    Benson Haynes Allen

Charles W. (Chuck) Miller
Mary Jane Allen Miller
    Charles W. (Chuck) Miller, Jr.
    Carolyn Kay (Carrie) Miller
    John O'Brien Miller

I
Autobiography

ONE DAY I walked into the chapel at Young Harris College and saw a black-haired girl on the stage playing a violin. When I saw her, I said, "Lord, that's the one for me." Her name was Leila Jane Haynes and she grew up in Clermont, Georgia. We courted for four years. During that time I saved up fifty-five dollars and decided that it was time for us to get married. I spent twenty-five dollars on her wedding ring which she proudly wears to this day. In the meantime, she had been teaching school and she had saved a hundred dollars. I told her that she should keep her hundred dollars and use it for special things as we went along. But she insisted that we would always share equally. So she put her hundred dollars together with my thirty. That was the smartest decision she ever made. During these forty-two years, we have still been sharing equally, and that is the last money she ever put in.

Next to the salvation of my soul and my birth, marrying Leila was the most important thing and the best thing that ever happened in my life. Our years together have been my greatest blessing.

During these years, I have spent a lot of time traveling about the country preaching. To some people, that kind of a life seems a bit glamorous—but really—it is about the loneliest life one can spend. Night after night after night, I have preached in churches and in auditoriums that were filled to overflowing and then go back to some strange motel room. After so long, you almost forget what town you are in and you feel like you have lost your identity. I never shall forget an experience that I had in Orlando, Florida. I was staying at a very lovely hotel. One afternoon I was walking down the sidewalk and I saw coming toward me the hotel maid, who had been cleaning my room that week. I did not speak to her, but as we drew closer I saw a smile of recognition on her face. (I think she was not quite sure who I was.) Just as she got by me she stopped and turned and said, "I know who you are—you are Number 106." I thought then that when people begin identifying you just by the room in which you are staying, you are not very important. But later on, I had an even more humiliating experience. I was preaching in Memphis, Tennessee. One morning I walked into the coffee shop and the waitress said to me, "I know you—you are one scrambled egg with bacon and hold the grits." Experiences like those took a lot of the glamour out this traveling business!

Every night that I have been away from home during the years of our marriage, I have telephoned Leila. I wanted never to let a day pass without talking to her. Perhaps the most unusual call I ever made was one from London. Rabbi Hyman Judah Schachtel (rabbi for more than a third of a century of Houston's largest Jewish Temple) and I were in Paris together. We got on the plane to come home, but engine trouble developed and we turned back and landed in London. It was necessary for us to spend the night there and get another plane the next day. Since Leila was expecting me home that night, I felt she would be worried about me. So

I put in a telephone call to her. The call was late getting through and finally about one o'clock, the phone rang and I talked to her. But during the process I woke up Rabbi Schachtel. The next morning I apologized for waking him up and he replied, "It's all right, Charles. For nearly twenty centuries the Christians have been persecuting the Jews." If I were naming my best friends, the rabbi would be one of them. But I still persecute him every so often.

Someone once asked my wife, Leila, if she ever felt the call to preach. Her reply was "Yes. God called me to preach and He gave me a very small congregation. Their names are Charles Junior, Franklin, and Mary Jane." I will say she has done a better job with her congregation than I ever did with mine.

Every so often my wife was asked how she felt about being moved from one church to another. She told people that she said to me, "Whither thou goest—you have to take me."

Those three children are all grown now and we never had one serious problem with any one of them during all of the years. One of the things I am happiest about is that we never lost communication with our children. Three of the events that we cherish so much are their weddings. Each of them had a full church wedding and they were beautiful. At Mary Jane's wedding, the entire choir of the church sang. Later, one of the church members said to me, "It is amazing how far some people will go to keep from having to pay a wedding soloist." Mary Jane wanted me to perform the ceremony, but I told her that I could perform hundreds and hundreds of marriage ceremonies, but I only had one chance to be the father of the bride—and I did not intend to miss that chance. She married Chuck Miller from Tulsa, Oklahoma. Charles, Jr., married Kay deMange from Charleston, Mississippi, and Franklin married Anne Woolridge from Corpus Christi,

Texas. If I had made the selections myself, I could not have done better. In fact, I believe I love and appreciate my in-law children even better than the originals.

Two of the boys hold important executive positions in large corporations. One is the president of a bank in Houston. All our children are in church every Sunday, and are very active in some phase of the church program. I really feel the fact that my children love the church is the highest compliment to my own ministry.

We have eight grandchildren. You remember about the man who said to his friend, "Have I told you about my grandchildren?" His friend replied, "No, and I sure do appreciate it."

As I think about marriage—and especially my own marriage—there are three words that I feel are basically essential. One is *appreciation*. Leila and I have made each other feel appreciated by the other. Someone once wrote to Dorothy Dix asking the question, "How can I hold the love of my husband?" Her reply was very wise: "Learn a hundred ways of saying, 'I think you are wonderful.'" Leila did that and I'll love her for it until I die.

Perseverance is the second word that I feel is so important in marriage. Certainly Edgar A. Guest was right when he said, "It takes a heap o' livin' in a house t' make it home." When two people marry they should be in love, and that romantic love is thrilling and beautiful. But that first love cannot be compared in strength and quality to the love that is developed as through the years those same two people "share each other's woes, each other's burdens bear," as the favorite old hymn "Blest Be the Tie That Binds" declares.

Up in the mountains of North Georgia, I once heard a boy give a definition of love. I still think it is the best definition I ever heard. He said:

Love is two hearts that yearn for one sweet presence,
Where his'n is her'n and her'n is his'n.

Love is not enough for marriage. Couples must dream and plan together. They must play and work together. They must spend their money and rear their children together. Little by little, they become one—inseparable—each finding completeness in the other.

The third word I mention as being so important in marriage is *prayer.* We remember the words of Christ: ". . . What therefore God hath joined together . . ." (Matthew 19:6). Marriage is a spiritual experience and it must be kept on that plane.

Speaking of marriage, I could fill the remainder of these pages remembering my mother. However, I will not be writing as much about her as I will be recalling my father. Papa was a preacher, and I have been a preacher, so it has been natural for me to pretty much pattern after him. But my mother was a wonderful and remarkable woman. My mother married when she was sixteen; therefore she had very little formal education and yet she became a very educated woman. She had a burning desire for her children to become educated. I do not understand it, because my father made very poor salaries—but all seven of her living children graduated from college. We got fourteen college degrees among us. I really feel that my mother put within us the ambition that we needed. She was proud of each one of her children, including me.

After she died, I found among her papers a number of newspaper notices about me. I remembered the story of Robert Louis Stevenson. Looking at the pages of a scrapbook his mother had kept about him, a friend said to him jokingly, "Is fame all it's cracked up to be?" "Yes," he answered, "when

I see my mother's face."

My mother's last years were spent in Houston, and I shall never forget seeing her sitting in the congregation of my church. It would be utterly impossible to describe the pride and joy she felt seeing her son in that pulpit. She really was a wonderful woman.

Somewhere I read that Leslie Weatherhead said that he was at his height—both mentally and spiritually—when he was sixty-two years old. That is my age as I write this, and I think maybe that inspired me to write this book, which I think of as my *Autobiography*. I decided that maybe if I wrote it now, I'd do better than if I waited. So—here it is. Naturally, this type of writing is an "*I*-book," but I shall do my best not to brag too much. The thing that bothers me the most is, there are so many people that I would like to talk about, but space does not permit even the listing of those names. I feel that most of those people know their names are written in my heart and in my love, and will forgive me for leaving them out of these pages. However, I must mention here my special appreciation to Mrs. Constance Ward, my secretary, for her valuable assistance in preparing this manuscript.

I guess the two biggest breaks of my ministry were moving to Grace United Methodist Church in Atlanta when I was thirty-five years old, and getting the chance to write a regular newspaper column for the *Atlanta Journal* and later the *Atlanta Constitution*. Grace Church gave me the chance to get before a great city. Writing the newspaper column made me work at writing. I shall always be grateful for those opportunities.

Also, when I first went to Atlanta I began a radio program on WSB which lasted for twelve years. But the thing I appreciate even more, was the chance at television. I remember talking to John Outler, who was in charge of WSB Radio and Television. He was the brother of the distinguished Dr. Albert Outler of Perkins School of Theology. I wanted my church service to be televised, but John insisted that a church service would not go over on television. We kept talking and finally he let me try it. As far as I can determine, I had the first regular church service ever televised in the United States. That was in 1949. I have been preaching on television ever since, both in Atlanta and in Houston. It is a thrilling experience to realize that you are preaching to perhaps a quarter of a million people every Sunday. But it is also a fearsome responsibility.

Each Sunday my morning church service is broadcast on Radio Station KENR, Houston. (This is really one of the happy stories of my ministry.) One day a man I had never seen before walked into my office. He told me that his name was William J. Edwards, and that he lived in Saginaw, Michigan. He said he was beginning a new radio station in Houston and wanted my church service on that station every Sunday. I asked what it would cost and he replied, "Not one cent." He even told me they would pay the telephone line charges! Then I asked why he was making me that offer, and he told me this: "Several years ago I read one of your books. That book made a great impression on my life and I said then —if I ever had the chance—I wanted the man who wrote that book to be on my radio station." I will always hold with deep appreciation William J. Edwards.

And this leads me to a chapter of my life for which I am grateful to God—the writing of my books. My books came about in this way: I was writing a column for the *Atlanta Journal*. One day I read Frank C. Laubach's little book entitled *Prayer, the Mightiest Force in the World*. That book inspired me greatly. I went to the Cokesbury Bookstore in

Atlanta and told them that if they would order a thousand copies of that book, I would write it up in my newspaper column and that I would also talk about it on my radio program that Sunday. They ordered the thousand copies and placed them on display in the store. The newspaper column and the radio braodcast took place on Sunday. And the next day every one of those thousand copies was sold! That book was published by Fleming H. Revell Company, and they suddenly began getting orders for that book from every bookstore in Georgia. They wondered what had happened, and Mr. William R. Barbour, Sr., came down to Atlanta to see. He was the head man of the Revell Company for many years. Soon afterwards he brought in Wilbur H. Davies, whom I have loved as much as any man I have ever known. Now the company is being run by Mr. Barbour's sons, Bill, Jr., and Hugh. During the years I have had offers from many publishers, but my relationship with Revell has been so happy and so satisfactory, that I never expect to change. Anyway—back to my story.

Mr. Barbour found out that the reasons for the unusual sale of the Laubach book were my column and radio broadcast. He called me and I went down to his hotel and drove him out to the airport. On the way he asked if I might have a manuscript. I sent the material that made up the book *Roads to Radiant Living*. That was my first book, and I am happy to say it is still selling today. During these last twenty-five years, this is the twenty-seventh book which I have written that Revell has published. The sales have now gone past the three million mark. My books have been published in Great Britain, translated into Spanish, Finnish, Portuguese, German, Dutch, Chinese, and Korean, and sold around the world. Without doubt, my books have been my widest ministry. Nearly every one of them is still in print and is being sold (with the exception of three little Christmas books and one other). I am hoping the publisher will one day republish those Christmas books in one larger Christmas book. I think it would have a good sale.

We moved to the First Methodist Church in Houston in 1960. This church is located in the very center of the downtown section. Nearly every downtown church is losing members and most of them have fled to the suburbs. I never shall forget when one of the members of our church phoned me and said that he would be by in a few minutes—that he wanted me to go with him. I was waiting on the corner when he came by. He drove out to a very lovely spot in the center of Southwest Houston. He pointed out ten very valuable acres of land at a most desirable location. He told me that he wanted to give First Methodist Church those ten acres of land and a check for a million dollars—and he wanted us to move out there and build a new church. I suggested he give us the land and money, and we would see about it later but he was too wise for that. He told me that we must either accept the offer and build the new church immediately, or else he would withdraw it. I think that day I made the wisest decision I have ever made as a minister. I did not discuss it with anybody else in the church. I just took the responsibility myself. I told this dear friend that there were plenty suburban churches, but if a church moved from the downtown area it could never move back because the property would be unobtainable. I told him that I felt our church should remain downtown and so it has.

I am now in my sixteenth year as pastor of the church. During these sixteen years I have seen the membership grow from six thousand to eleven thousand. I expect to see it continue to grow. People will come downtown if a church gives them what they are seeking.

During these sixteen years, we have completely renovated our church building. When I say *renovated,* I really mean almost reconstructed. We tore out nearly every wall inside the building and rebuilt. It is a better building today than when it was first built in 1910.

Really, the renovation of the building started in this way: Mrs. Mildred Parker came to First Church as Director of Christian Education. (Parenthetically, I would like to say that I have never known any director as good as she is.) She had not been there long until she told me that she wanted to repaint one of the nursery rooms. I suggested that we had an architect named Mr. Ed Reichert and that he would be glad to work with her and give her some advice. Well—to make a long story short—repainting that nursery resulted in spending $2,700,000 in renovating the building. (Today, the same job would cost twice as much.) As I write these words, the church owes less than $200,000 to pay for the entire job (which the church could pay in one Sunday if it wanted to). But there the church stands, and there it will continue to stand for generations to come.

As I look back over the years of my ministry, I am painfully aware that I have constantly suffered from feelings of unworthiness and inadequacy. The first sermon I preached I felt very inadequate. I have had that same feeling every time I have ever preached. There have been Sundays when I felt I just did not have enough strength to walk up the steps into the pulpit. At times I have been judged to be very confident and self-assured—but such is not the case. I have felt very unworthy. Even so, I have given it my best and will continue to do so.

I have never been too interested in church history. I appreciate the past, but I am living in the present and I am planning for the future. I feel that I pattern my ministry after the way I drive my car—I spend more time looking through the windshield than I do the rear-view mirror.

Twice Saint Paul uses a phrase "according to my gospel" (*see* Romans 2:16; 16:25). Of course, our mission is to preach the Gospel of Christ, but no preacher has the wisdom and understanding to preach all of the Gospel. Christ is so great and so beyond any of the rest us that no Christian preacher can ever hope to really adequately preach the Gospel of Christ. Instead, we each have to preach it as we see it and as we understand it. And so, what follows I feel I can reverently say is "according to my gospel."

II

What I Believe

I
Belief—The Golden Thread

THE MOST IMPORTANT thing about me is what I believe. That is true for every person. I have heard someone say, "It is not what you believe but how you live that matters." That is not true because what you believe determines how you live. What you believe determines what you are. Your belief determines the power of your life. On one occasion Jesus said, ". . . all things are possible to him that believeth" (Mark 9:23). Your belief determines the possibilities of your life.

Journalist Claud M. Bristol asked this question: "Is there a something, a force, a factor, a power, a science—call it what you will—which a few people understand and use to overcome their difficulties and achieve outstanding success?"

As a newspaper reporter, Mr. Bristol studied the religions of the world and watched them operate. In hospitals he saw people die, but others get well who were just as sick. He watched football teams win while other teams, which had just as good material, would lose. He studied the lives of the great men and women of history; he met and interviewed the outstanding men and women in all lines of human endeavor. As a result of years of study, he said:

... Gradually I discovered that there is a golden thread that runs through all the teachings and makes them work for those who sincerely accept and apply them, and that thread can be named in a single word—belief. It is the same element or factor, belief, which causes people to be cured through mental healing, enables others to climb higher the ladder of success ... there's genuine magic in believing ....

So, he wrote a book which is still available: *The Magic of Believing.*

Long before Mr. Bristol wrote his book, the great psychologist William James arrived at the same conclusion. He said, "Our belief at the beginning of a doubtful undertaking is the one thing that assures the successful outcome of our venture." Notice he said *the one thing.*

Long before William James lived, Jesus Christ said the same thing, and I repeat: "If thou canst believe, all things are possible to him that believeth." It is amazing what a belief can accomplish.

The word *belief* is a big, strong, compelling word. It is not simply giving assent to what someone else has said. It does not mean shutting our eyes to the truth and clinging to a dream. We have opinions and we have notions, but belief is a *conviction.* A conviction is something that makes one a convict. It chains them, and binds them, and imprisons them. When you are gripped by a belief you are not free anymore. Your belief becomes the controlling force in your life.

When it comes to my religious faith, I have asked myself what are really my beliefs—not what has somebody told me to believe—but rather what do I, myself, *really* believe. I have listed eight basic beliefs that I wish to discuss here. Of course, I could have listed many others, but I feel these are the basic eight. In other pages of this book I discuss my beliefs about some other subjects. Across the years, I have found oftentimes that good and sincere people have disagreed with me at some point. It never worries me if somebody has a different opinion from mine. The important thing is, that each one of us determines what he believes for himself. In listing the principles of my own faith, perhaps it will help you to decide your faith.

2
I Believe in the Bible

I PUT THAT first, not because I think it is the most important, but rather because the Bible is our textbook. The Bible is our chief source of knowledge about God. I know people say they can see God in nature, or in history, or in the lives of other people, or in the world in which we live, and even in the stars in the sky. But were it not for the revelation of God that we have in the Bible, we would not see Him in these other ways.

I believe the Bible is different from any other writing in this world. I believe it to be the *inspired* word of God. There is a story that Columbus and his men sailed into the mouth of the Amazon River. One of the men said to Columbus, "We have discovered an island." But when Columbus looked at that river he said, "No, we have discovered a continent. A river that big could not come from an island."

I am familiar with the various theories as to how God inspired the Scripture, but I really am not concerned about how He did it. The important thing is, He *did* do it. The Bible did not come just from the minds of man. A book that great had to come through the inspiration of God.

One of the characters in *Alice in Wonderland* is a lock. I presume it was an ordinary padlock. This lock was very restless. It could not be still even for a moment. It was always running around looking behind every stone, stump, and tree. It was always hunting for something. As Alice watched it, her curiosity was aroused, and she asked, "What is the matter?"

The lock replied, "I am seeking for something to unlock me."

To me that represents the Bible down through the centuries. Again and again, it has been a restless book, seeking for somebody to unlock it.

That was one of the main tasks of our Lord on earth. He said, "Think not that I am come to destroy the law, or the prophets: I am not come to destroy, but to fulfil" (Matthew 5:17).

Religious leaders of His day had locked the Bible tight with a thousand petty laws and regulations. The Bible in that day was like a mountain peak hidden by clouds, or fertile fields grown over in weeds and briars. Jesus came to drive the clouds away, or clear the ground so it could be seen.

The evidence of His life teaches us that He carefully studied the Bible. He refused to listen merely to what men said about it. He learned for Himself. And when He went forth to preach, He preached the Bible. Practically everything He said had already been written in the Bible of that day. He took the Bible of that day and made it live anew by His pure life and the simplicity of His interpretations. Jesus was a divine key that unlocked the Bible.

Later on we find the Bible locked again. Locked by the church, which maintained that only the ordained priest had a right of access to the printed page of the Bible. God sent Martin Luther, who again became a key that unlocked the Bible. The Bible is constantly being locked. In Revelation, Saint John says, "And I saw in the right hand of him that sat on the throne a book written within and on the backside, sealed with seven seals" (5:1). Constantly the Bible is a book sealed.

Today it is not locked by language, for as Charles Wesley wrote, "O for a thousand tongues to sing." Today the Bible is translated in nearly every known tongue of man. We have available to us many different translations. One of the most inspiring experiences I have had as a preacher came several years ago when I selected thirty-one different versions of chapter 13 First Corinthians. I put them in a little pamphlet and sent it out to the people of my own church—with the request that they read one each day for the month. Then, during that month, I preached on the meaning of love. Later I published those versions and my sermons in a book entitled *The Miracle of Love*. It was thrilling to search through the various translations of the Bible and pick out the thirty-one that I thought were the best. There are many translations today that give us new insights into the Word of God. The Bible is not locked by language.

Neither is the Bible locked by governmental decree, nor by scarcity, nor by scorn, or unbelief, or ridicule. The Bible is not locked by being out of date, but there are *seven* seals on the Bible today for many people. Let me briefly mention them.

One is the *lock of mystery*. To many people the Bible is a glorified puzzle or riddle. To them every word has some hidden or mysterious meaning. For example, consider how some people study that beautiful story of the shepherd that had a hundred sheep and lost one of them. It is a story that is sublime because of the utter simplicity. But some people ruin it by giving some mysterious meaning to the fact that there were a hundred sheep. It really doesn't matter whether he had a hundred or a thousand. The real message is simply that the shepherd was anxious to find his sheep that was lost.

To some people the number 666 in Revelation means more

than the Twenty-third Psalm. To many the Bible is not a means of grace; rather is it a bag of tricks to be solved by someone that possesses a peculiar key.

I know there are parts of the Bible that are difficult to understand. But as I read the Bible, I many times think of the words of General Booth. He said that he read his Bible as he ate fish. He ate the meat and laid the bones aside. Or, I think of the words of Mark Twain, when someone said to him that he did not read the Bible because there was so much he could not understand.

Mark Twain replied, "What bothers me in the Bible is not what I do not understand, but what I do understand."

The Bible tells us how to live and how to die. How to suffer and how to succeed. How to conquer the world and how to get along with our fellowmen. These are important things and you do not need to understand every word of the Bible to learn the truth. Mainly, the Bible tells us what God is like and that's what it's for.

Sometimes we lock the Bible *when we make it a parlor book*. Modern homes today do not have parlors, because that was the silliest room in the house. In the old days the shades of the parlor were kept tightly drawn. It was a cold, unfriendly room, and it was hardly open except when some important person came to visit. One of the main ornaments on the big table in the parlor was the Bible. There it was— a closed book in a cold, clammy parlor.

Then we lock the Bible *when we make it a fetish*. A fetish is something that is supposed to have some sort of magic power within itself. I have seen witnesses in court asked to place their hand on the Bible and swear to tell the truth. The idea was that putting your hand on the Bible would make you more honest, which is silly. To some people, the Bible is sort of a charm, or a good luck piece, or a glorified rabbit foot—something to keep with you but not read.

Others, lock the Bible *by making it sort of a holy encyclopedia*—an answer book for all religious arguments. The Bible *does* contain the solutions of the problems of your life. John 14 has dried the tears of many eyes. Psalm 51 has brought sinful hearts to God in humble repentance. Isaiah 40 has encouraged the discouraged lives through the ages. Hebrews 11 has stirred the faith of multitudes. First Corinthians 13 has brought love to many bitter and cynical souls. Romans 12 has made religion real and practical to thousands.

It *will* solve your problems, but first it must become your friend and companion. It must be approached as a book of God, rather than dictionary of meanings.

I think we lock the Bible *when we make it a grab bag of texts.* The Bible is not just a book of quotations. It is said that one can prove anything by the Bible—that is, by lifting up verses out of context. But really, the Bible is one great story, beginning with the first word in Genesis to the last word in Revelation. Greatness of the Bible is not in its isolated statements, but in its one great picture of God.

Another way we lock the Bible is *assuming that it is a dull or uninteresting book*—a book that is our duty to read, but really, is not something we would enjoy. But no book that is dull and uninteresting can do what the Bible has done. It has lifted empires off their hinges. It has shaped the course of human history. It has molded the lives of multiplied millions of people. It is a constant best seller. It is only reasonable to suppose that the pages of the Bible contain a story both thrilling and powerful.

Finally, we lock the Bible *when we fail to realize it is a timeless book.* "The heavens declare the glory of God . . ." (Psalms 19:1). That statement is just as true today as it was thousands of years ago. The Bible is as fresh and as modern and as new as any book that exists.

As Christians, we should read the Bible. I would like to suggest three ways it should be read.

First, *it should be read without trying to find fault with it.* I will never forget the first time I saw the girl that later became my wife. I might have said to her, "The earring on your left ear is crooked." I might have said that, but I did not. The truth is I did not notice whether she had on an earring or not. I do not remember whether she was wearing a red dress or a blue dress. I did not see a lot of details about her—I just saw her. In seeing her, I fell in love with her.

I shall never forget the first time I saw the ocean. I just stood and looked at as much of it as my eyes could take in. I did not stop to analyze the water to see if it had a proper mixture of hydrogen and oxygen—or to see how much salt it contained. I just looked at the ocean, and my heart was lifted by the very greatness of what I saw.

Likewise, when I read the Bible, I do not stop to argue about every word or every verse. There is just something glorious about seeing what it contains and when you see it you come to love it and be conquered by it.

In the second place, *the Bible should be read with imagination.* I like to let my mind carry me back across the centuries and let me become one of those who were actually present in the days of the flesh of our Lord. I like to hear the big, booming voice of John the Baptist, as he said, ". . . There cometh one mightier than I after me, the latchet of whose shoes I am not worthy to stoop down and unloose" (Mark 1:7). As I hear that voice I know John is not talking about some palefaced, anemic, goody-goody, weak, and flabby person. He is talking about One who is great and powerful, and One I am anxious to meet, and to know, and to have fellowship with.

Then in the third place, *the Bible should be read with one's heart as well as with his mind.* Really, as I read the Word of God, I am not seeking information so much as inspiration. I am not seeking to learn history so much as I am to meet a Person.

As a preacher, I feel it is my responsibility to preach the Bible. It is the business of a church to teach the Bible. It is the duty of a Christian to read the Bible.

I believe in the Bible.

3
I Believe In God

QUICKLY I CAN list a dozen reasons why one believes in God. But as I look at those reasons, I know they are not my reasons for believing. My books on theology give the arguments for God, and studying these books strengthens my faith and confirms my beliefs. But what I read in my books is not the reason I believe. I could copy reasons from those books and give them as my reasons, but that would not be honest.

The fact is, I believed in God long before I ever studied theology. The more I think about it, the more I realize that I believed before I ever knew any of the reasons *for* believing. I know now that it is necessary for me to breathe and that without air I would die. But long before I knew that—I just breathed.

I was born in a home where prayer was heard regularly. I did not question if there was a God to hear those prayers. I just accepted the fact. I was carried to church, and it has always seemed normal and right for me to go to church. Long before I knew how the church came to be, or the reasons for its existence, I felt at home in it. In an American court of law a person is presumed to be innocent until he is proven guilty. So it is with my own belief in God. Instead of saying I will not believe until God's existence is proven, I simply believe, and will continue to believe, until it is proven that God does not exist. Up to now, I have never had any cause to doubt the existence of God; thus, I have never felt the necessity of trying to prove Him.

Certainly the Bible never felt the necessity for proving the existence of God. The very first words of the Bible are "In the beginning God. . . ." Then the Bible goes on to give us a progressive revelation of God. I feel that God took care of our beliefs when He created us. We may call it instinct, insight, intuition, or by any other name, but I think we were just born believing. To be a nonbeliever is unnatural. The Ten Commandments do not command us to believe because it is not necessary to make that command.

Some time ago, a worshiper in the church where I minister said to me, "Please tell me how I can believe in God." This person went on to say, "You talk about God as if everybody knew Him, but I need to know who He is, where He is, or what He does. As far as I know, I have never had any conscious dealing with God. In your sermons you say, 'Put your life in God's hands and He will carry you through.' That is like saying to one who has never flown a plane, 'Get into that plane and fly it wherever you want to go.' I do not doubt the plane's existence, or its ability to carry me, but I do know I cannot fly. As for God, I am not even sure that He exists and certainly I do not know how to 'put my life in His hands.' "

In seeking an answer to that request I turned to the ninth chapter of Saint Mark's Gospel. Jesus and three of His disciples went up on the mountain and there had a marvelous experience. In fact, they wanted just to stay in that lofty spiritual atmosphere. But Jesus knew there were needs to be met in the valley below. God never gives His power to those who will not use it in service to mankind. At the foot of the mountain was a father who had brought his sick son to Jesus. Since childhood the boy had been afflicted, probably with epilepsy. He asked Jesus to heal the boy.

Jesus said, "If thou canst believe, all things are possible to him that believeth" (v. 23). Stop for a moment at that word *believe*. In our language it has at least three meanings. A person may say, "I believe in the North Pole." He may not have been there, but he accepts the authority of one who has been there.

Another person may say, "I believe that 2 times 2 is 4." That is something that he can reason out and prove for himself. Thus, his belief is based on his own intellect.

Another says, "I believe the sunshine is warm." He has been in the sunshine and felt it. Thus, his belief is based on his experience. He cannot explain why the sunshine is warm, but he knows it is.

The belief in God that matters most is not just the accepting of the authority of somebody else—nor mere intellectual reasoning—but rather, it is the experience that one has with God.

The father in Mark 9:24 says, "Lord, I believe; help thou mine unbelief." That is, he believes, but his belief is not perfect or complete. He still has some difficulties in believing. Perhaps one reason for his unbelief is the fact that he had been disappointed so many times. Ever since this son of his was a little child, the father had carried him to doctors; he had left no stone unturned in seeking the healing of the boy. Time after time he was disappointed. It is easy to believe when everything is going well, but when our lives are blocked at every turn, then belief is much more difficult. During my ministry I have talked with many people who had genuine doubts about the existence of God, and I have found that in every instance it was a person with whom life had dealt harshly.

A person can have piled up in life just so many sorrows and disappointments, and frustrations, and bitternesses; then, after a while, the burden gets so heavy that it is difficult to carry. When that happens, it is normal and natural to begin doubting—not only the existence of God—but the existence of anything that is good. The Bible tells us, ". . . hope thou in God . . ." (Psalms 42:5). But it is possible for the burden of sorrow and disappointment to become so great that one can see no hope—and losing hope—we lose God.

Time after time as people have come to see me to talk about God, I have instead insisted that they talk about themselves. As we talked about the burdens of their own lives, I have seen new belief and faith creeping in. When you are with a person who disbelieves in God, your first step is not to talk about God, but rather, you should put a warming friendship about him or her, and help in some way to lift the burden.

We cannot prove God by argument, but we *can* make our own lives an argument for God. Discouragement is often the beginning of doubt and unbelief. Encouragement is usually the doorway to God's presence. This father in the ninth chapter of Saint Mark's Gospel had a son who was crippled. He could not play as other boys could play. If he was left alone in the house, there was a possibility he might fall into the fire. He could not look forward to a normal manhood. Probably it would be hard for him to make a living, yet this boy had done no wrong. He was completely innocent.

His father had been told that God made us and that God was good. If that is true, then how could you explain why a good God would make an afflicted child? Why would God allow a person to suffer all through life, especially when that person had done nothing to deserve it?

Here is even a greater problem. Not only do we become concerned about belief in God, but also about the character of God. Better to have no God, if He is a bad God. But if we claim a Creator God who is good, how can we explain afflictions and all the evil in the world? If I slipped in in the night and set your house on fire, I would be convicted of crime. Yet, again and again, bolts of lightning come from the sky and burn up people's homes. If I set off a dynamite charge under your home and killed you, it would be murder. Yet the earthquakes come which kill in wholesale quantities. It is hard to explain a good God and the existence of evil, and that is one reason why it is hard to believe.

Suppose, however, because of evil we decide not to believe in God. Then we have before us an even greater problem. How can we explain the goodness in the world if there is no God? For example, one can go to Calvary and if he centers his attention on the cross with all of its pain and suffering, he might conclude there is no God. One of the thieves who died by Jesus' side did just that. "If thou be Christ . . ." he said (Luke 23:39). It was really a sneer—an expression of unbelief. But the man on the other side of Christ fixed his attention, not on the cross, but on the Christ. As he saw Him, he began to believe and said, "Lord, remember me . . ." (Luke 23:42). A man standing by was heard to say, ". . . Truly, this was the Son of God" (Matthew 27:54).

When we concentrate on the crosses of our own lives, it does make for unbelief. Storms, earthquakes, and diseases produce more despair than faith. But on the other hand, how do we explain sunsets and music, mothers and laughter, flowers and victories—if we leave out the existence of a good God?

Sure, there is evil in the world. Why it is here and from whence it came, is not easy to explain—but let us never forget that God can and does overcome evil. Faith in God gives us a daring confidence. One does not need to understand God in order to believe in Him. Most of us do not understand the composition of water, but we drink it. None of us know what electricity is, but we use it. Who can understand the process of life, yet many have given their lives in sacrifice because they have loved.

I like the story of the little girl who asked her father the question, "What was God doing last night during the storm?" Then she answered her own question: "I know. God was making the morning." So it is with the storms of our own lives. God is forever making mornings.

No person ever really believes in God, until he or she feels the need for God. We trust in God because of our own weaknesses and inadequacies.

Another thought we need to remember is, no person believes in all of God. God is so great and we are so small, that we can only believe in a part of Him. I have a little home overlooking the Gulf of Mexico. I like to sit on the porch and look out across the water. As far as I can see there is water. I can walk down to the beach and swim in the water. I can taste the salt in it. I have a little sailboat in which I can sail out across the waves. I believe in the ocean, because I have seen it and felt it. But, I have not seen all of the ocean. I have not been with Admiral Byrd to the Arctic and the Antarctic. I have not been to the tropic ocean where the Amazon pours its flood out so freely. In the ocean there are many mountain ranges higher and longer than any man has ever seen. There are canyons in the ocean deeper than the dry earth knows of. There are vast land areas on the earth, but the sea is three times larger than the land areas of the earth. Any person could spend a lifetime studying the sea and know only a small part of it at the end of the study. But, though we do not know it all, still with assurance we say, "I believe in the sea."

I can say I believe in people. Yet, I base that belief on a very limited acquaintance. There is my immediate family, my close friends, people I work with in the church, and people I have met along the way. But if I were to add up all the people I have ever known, when I finished, it would be a very small percentage of the 4 billion people on the earth today. Yet in the people I do know, I have seen love and faith, loyalty and unselfishness, goodness and integrity, to the extent that I can firmly say, "I believe in people." I do not have to know every person before I can say that I believe in people.

So I believe in God. He is so great that I can never know Him, yet He is so near that I cannot help but know Him. The Bible tells us, ". . . God is love" (1 John 4:8). I have loved and I have been loved. I have seen love in its best in many ways. Seeing and feeling love, I have come to believe in it. Believing in love is believing in God—a small part of God, to be sure—but still God.

The Bible speaks of the beauty of God. Beauty is God. Not all of God, but certainly part of Him. I watch the rainbow. I gaze upon the face of a tiny, blue violet. I hear the psalmist as he prays, "And let the beauty of the LORD our God be upon us . . ." (Psalms 90:17). And I see people for whom that prayer has been answered. I have not seen all of the beauty there is, but I have seen enough to know it exists. Thus, I know there is a God, because beauty is a part of God.

Each day we can know a little more of God. We can never know all of Him, but instead of worrying about the part of God I do not know, I say, "Lord, I believe; help me to believe more completely." This man whose son was sick might have become so bitter that he would never have come in search of

Christ. But, he did come. If we concentrate on our tragedies, it will destroy our belief. On the other hand, the struggle to overcome the sorrow and evil we face is at the same time a struggle to find God.

Many books have been written to explain suffering, and there is at least a three-fold explanation for it. Some suffering is caused by the "law-abidingness" of the universe. God made certain laws, and if we break them, it hurts us. There is the law of gravitation. If I jump out of a high window, I will hurt myself. The law of gravitation will not be changed just because I do not wish to obey it. God made certain laws for me to live by. As someone put it, "No one breaks the law alone; he breaks himself, but never the law." Much of man's suffering is caused by his disobedience to God.

I was speaking on the campus of one of our largest universities recently. One afternoon I was meeting with a small group. One of the students described a pattern of life that he was following. And then he said to me, "If I want to live like this, why can't I do it?" I told him that he could not live that way because God said he could not do it. There is such a thing as sin. Sin is breaking the law of God, and sin brings suffering. There is no doubt about it.

Much of the suffering of the world is brought about because the world is constantly in a changing state. Life is all the time fighting its way upward. Ignorance, poverty, and all the limitations of this life are constantly being fought against and conquered. But the fighting to better ourselves is not easy. Yet as we look at man today and trace back his progress down through history, we see that gradually the good is overcoming the evil. We are reminded of the words in Maltbie D. Babcock's hymn "This Is My Father's World": "That though the wrong seems oft so strong, God is the Ruler yet." The very progress of civilization is a reason for belief in God. We suffer because our lives are intermeshed and interrelated with each other. We are members of one another. If someone else is hurt, it hurts us. That, too, is a reason for believing. Our very suffering because of others is proof of brotherhood, and brotherhood is proof of a fatherhood, and that fatherhood is God.

But if you said to me, "What must I believe?" I would not argue intellectual propositions with you; rather, I would tell you to do as the father of the afflicted child did. Come and talk with Jesus about it. Accept His friendship as best you understand it. *Faith never becomes real until it becomes personal.*

There is something else I want to say about my belief in God. Not only did He make the laws by which we live, He also loves us. We are His children. Over and over, I have said to my children, "If you ever get in trouble, I want to be the first person you call." That does not mean I would condone anything one of my children did. It *does* mean that no matter what one of my children might do, I would still be his or her father, and I would still love each of them and help them.

For many years, I have been the pastor of a large church in the heart of a big city. About once a month, a girl who is in trouble will come in to see me. They are usually nervous and embarrassed, and very hesitant. One came in the other day—about nineteen years old. She told me that she was not married, but that she is going to have a baby. She was almost panicky and had come to me for help. I said to her, "This is not the end of the world," and I assured her that we could help her and things could work out. "But," I said, "the first thing we must do is tell your father." She immediately protested. She explained to me that the reason she came to me was because she couldn't tell him. But I insisted there was no other way. Finally she gave me his phone number. I called him. He was a man I did not know. I said to him something like this, "Mr. ———, your daughter is sitting here in my

office. In the next few moments I am going to find out if you
are worthy to be her father." If that man would not help his
daughter when she needed it and was in trouble, then I say
he was not a worthy father.

I believe in a God who is a worthy God—a God who loves
me and will help me.

4
I Believe in Jesus Christ

LET'S BEGIN with the question "Who is Jesus?" That is a
thrilling, yet difficult question. In seeking an answer to that
question, I could very easily turn to my books and read what
many others have said about Him. But as I faced that question, I felt impressed just to sit for a time and think about
Him. One by one, the pictures of Him in my mind began
coming into view. I saw a lovely young mother sitting in a
stable by a manger. I heard a baby cry. I saw a young man
living in a tiny village. I saw this young man growing up and
taking on family responsibilities. He was about thirty years
of age when He went out and began to preach. For three
years He walked about the countryside and talked to the
people who would listen. He must have been a lonely man,
though He made friends and at times was surrounded by
multitudes. Still, in every man there is a deep longing for a
home, for a woman he loves, for little children to call his
own. Jesus never had that. Just my own fellowship with Him
makes me know He is more than Jesus. I know He is Jesus
Christ.

I know of no person who really questions the fact that a
man named Jesus once lived in Galilee. We are familiar with
the records of His life (which exist) and the kind of a man

He was. And, as we come to know about His earthly life, we can say with Richard Gilder:

> If Jesus Christ is a man
> And only a man,—I say
> That of all mankind I cleave to him,
> And to him will cleave alway.

But as we come to know about Jesus even from the cold printed words of the four Gospels, we begin to feel a closeness to Him and love for Him, and He begins to have a strange power over us. We become sure—really sure—that He was more than just a man. And so, we can say again, with Richard Gilder:

> If Jesus Christ is a God—
> And only a God,—I swear
> I will follow him through heaven and hell,
> The earth, the sea, the air.
>   "The Song of a Heathen"

The strongest proof that Jesus is the Christ is not what He once did on earth, but what He does today. I profoundly believe in the miracles of Christ. I studied each one of them carefully, and I wrote a book entitled *The Touch of the Master's Hand,* which is still selling in the bookstores throughout the land. But, the great significance of the miracles is the fact that He still does them. There was a man who had sold the furniture in his little home to buy liquor, but then he became a Christian. One day a friend sneeringly said to him, "You don't really believe that yarn about Jesus turning the water into wine?" The man replied, "I'm an ignorant man. I don't know about water and wine. But I know this, that Jesus Christ turned liquor into furniture in my house.

And that is a good enough miracle for me."

A number of times I have sailed in a little boat on the Sea of Galilee, and, of course, I would think about Jesus stilling the storm on that sea. When I was there there was no storm and I saw no miracle. But through more than forty years as the pastor of a church, I have seen many, many people in whose hearts our Lord stilled the storm after some great sorrow, or hurt, or disappointment. I know He is still working His miracles.

Many years ago, I offered through a newspaper column I wrote, a small billfold-size picture of Christ. I was not prepared for the requests that I received, and eventually sent out more than a hundred thousand copies of that little picture. I received hundreds of letters as a result of those pictures. One man wrote me that he lost his billfold with a considerable sum of money in it. A few days later he received it in the mail with a note from the finder saying, "When I first found this I fully intended to keep the money. But when I looked at that picture of Christ, I had to send it back." Even a picture of Him does something to people. Of course, He was more than just a man.

There are four facts about Christ which I firmly believe:

First, *Christ was born without an earthly father.* His birth was different from that of any other person who has ever lived. He was not an actual man; He was supernatural. God sent an angel to a pure young woman who told her that she would give birth to the Son of the Highest. She was puzzled, and answered, "How shall this be, seeing I know not a man?" The angel told her that the Holy Ghost would be His Father. (*See* Luke 1:26–35.) He was God even before He was born.

Second, *when He lived on earth He had supernatural power.* The winds and the waves obeyed His voice. He could heal sickness; He could even raise the dead. He could take one little boy's lunch and feed a multitude of five thousand.

He could forgive sin; He could put a song into a broken heart; He could bring hope to the discouraged and strength to the weary. With Nicodemus I say, ". . . no man can do these miracles that thou doest, except God be with him" (John 3:2). He imparted power to others and it is still available to people today.

Third, *I believe that His death on the cross is my doorway to eternal life.* His cross is an example of sacrifice, and it is a revelation of God's love—but it is more—*much more.* That Friday, He did something that forever makes a difference in my relationship with God. For these first disciples it was "black Friday." Their leader was crucified. It seemed that God had forsaken His own. But, later on those disciples realized, as Saint Paul put it, ". . . God was in Christ, reconciling the world unto himself . . ." (2 Corinthians 5:19). And when people realized that, then they saw the cross—not as God's desertion of man—but as God's saving power. Then *black Friday* became *Good Friday.*

Fourth, *I believe that Christ rose from the dead, and His Resurrection is my assurance that there is life for me beyond the grave.* ". . . because I live," He said, "ye shall live also" (John 14:19). I love the life we have here, but I know in a little while someone will carry my body and bury it in the ground. There it will decay, but because I know Christ, I know that will not be the end of me. I shall live after death.

Jesus Christ is the most loved person that ever lived on this earth. I often ask myself why, and really, I think it's because He is our best friend.

An English publication offered the prize for the best definition of a friend. Many answers were received and the one that was given first prize was this: "A friend is one who comes in when the whole world goes out." That is a mighty good definition.

Young Joseph Scriven was deeply in love with a girl. They

planned to marry, but she was accidentally drowned. For months he was bitter and heartbroken. Later he had a deep experience of Christ in his heart, and he wrote these very familiar lines:

> What a friend we have in Jesus,
> All our sins and griefs to bear!

I think there is, however, a better definition of a friend. Once Henry Ford was having lunch with a man. Suddenly he asked the man this question, "Who is your best friend?" The man was not sure, and then Ford said, "I will tell you who your best friend is." He took out a pencil and wrote on the tablecloth this sentence: *Your best friend is he who brings out the best that is within you.*

Jesus had a way of making people believe two things about themselves. First, *I ought not to be the way I am.* Second, *I need not stay the way I am.*

In every one of us there is a mixture of the best and the worst. Every human heart is an unseen battlefield where the good and the bad are fighting it out. Sometimes one wins and sometimes the other wins. When the bad wins out, we are ashamed and disgusted with ourselves. But, when the good wins, we have a clean feeling inside, and we are filled with joy. We have proven ourselves to be real people. Jesus brings out our best and that is why we love Him so.

One of my best friends in the ministry is Dr. Asbury Lenox. Recently, he told me this story: A man came into his study to talk with him. He was of a different faith and a different theology. They talked, but they seemed not to find many points of agreement. The man got up to go, and as he was walking out the door, he turned and said to Dr. Lenox, "Preacher, we can get together on Jesus."

I know that Christian people have different opinions about things, but somehow, I also know that "we can get together on Jesus."

5
I Believe in the Holy Spirit

I FEEL SURE that my first awareness of the presence of the Holy Spirit came as a result of my dear father's benedictions. I can hear him now saying, "The grace of the Lord Jesus Christ, and the love of God, and the communion of the Holy [Spirit] be with you all. Amen" (2 Corinthians 13:14). That was the benediction my father always used, and I heard it from the time I was a tiny boy. It did not offend me in any way and I had no reason to doubt the existence of the Holy Spirit. But, the truth of the matter is, I never gave the attention to the third Person of the Trinity, that I did to the first two. I have not given nearly so much thought to the Holy Spirit as I have to God and to Jesus Christ. Three years ago, I felt an inspiration to really study about the Holy Spirit. In my spare time, I would read what my books had to say about the Holy Spirit. But after a while, I decided I would read *The Book.* I put away all the other books and sat down with my Bible and some sheets of paper and said to myself, "What does the Bible say about the Holy Spirit?" Really, this was one of the most fruitful and inspiring studies of my life. As a result of that study, I wrote a small book entitled *The Miracle of the Holy Spirit,* which was my last book published before this one. I have been extremely pleased over the response this book has received. I think every Christian would do well to study what the Bible has to say about the Holy

Spirit. I began with the fourteenth chapter of Saint John, especially the sixteenth verse: "And I will pray the Father, and he shall give you another Comforter, that he may abide with you for ever." I went back and read this in the Greek and really, I feel the word *Comforter* is not an adequate translation. The Revised Standard Version uses the word *Counselor.* But, neither is that word adequate. Other translators use such words as *Advocate, Helper, Intercessor, Teacher.* Each of these and many other words apply to the purpose and work of the Holy Spirit, but after I studied, I think really what Jesus said is simply, "And He shall give you another person." When Jesus came He came as a person. Even though the Holy Spirit does not have a physical body, He is no less a person. And so, we can—and do—sing "God in Three Persons, Blessed Trinity." Jesus fully expected and understood that the Holy Spirit would come and carry on God's work on this earth.

Our Lord said to His disciples, ". . . tarry ye in the city of Jerusalem, until ye be endued with power from on high" (Luke 24:49). They were not to go out and begin their work until *first* the Holy Spirit had descended upon them. Without the Spirit they were powerless. As Jesus said to them, "But ye shall receive power, after that the Holy [Spirit] is come upon you . . ." (Acts 1:8). Without the Spirit, the Christian witness is powerless.

So the disciples and a few friends—numbering a total of about a hundred and twenty—gathered together in an upper room to pray for the coming of the Holy Spirit. They prayed together for ten days. It must have seemed to them a long time, but they stayed with it. And then we read, "And suddenly there came a sound from heaven as of a rushing mighty wind, and it filled all the house where they were sitting. And there appeared unto them cloven tongues like as of fire, and it sat upon each of them" (Acts 2:2,3).

Fire is used as an emblem again and again throughout the Bible. It is a symbol both of destruction and creativity. There is the fire of anger and also the fire of love. There is the fire of sunshine, which gives light, and also the fire of the lightning—which destroys. The Pentecostal fires are a warming, creative experience. We speak of one as being "set on fire for God." Coldness and indifference are burned away, enthusiasm takes possession of one. The warmth of love pervades the emotions. Our beliefs become living forces. That is what happens when the Holy Spirit comes into a human life.

Also, fire is a symbol of purity. The Prophet Isaiah spoke of how the filth of the people shall be washed away by the "spirit of burning" (*see* Isaiah 4:4). When the Holy Spirit comes upon one, it is a much greater experience than moral reformation. It is a cleansing of the sin of one's soul.

The fire came in the form of tongues. It was not a shapeless flame. The tongue is the instrument to be used in the establishment of the faith. Person is to speak to person. ". . . ye shall be witnesses unto me . . ." (Acts 1:8). A witness is one who tells what he knows.

Now the Spirit has come. God came on earth not as the Creator, not as a baby born in Bethlehem, but as an experience within a human being. This is the *third* coming of the Lord. First, God came to create the earth; second, He came in the person of Christ; third, He came in the form of the Spirit.

The promise of the Baptism of the Spirit was to those first Christians, but it is *no less a promise to Christians today.* How can one receive the Baptism of the Spirit? The conditions today are the same as they were in the beginning.

First, *they committed their lives to the service of God.* (God never gives power to a person who will not use it.)

Second, *they believed the promise of the coming of the Spirit.* As they were assembled in that upper room, there was no talk of going back. There was no doubting. We need to remember that faith precedes experience.

Third, *they prayed for the Spirit to come.* "These all continued with one accord in prayer . . ." (Acts 1:14). Their prayer was not a device to persuade God to do something, but rather, it was a preparation which enabled God to do something. There are many things God would like to give us, but we are not in a mood or a position to receive them. In that upper room their hearts became prepared.

Fourth, *they waited.* God does not always do things when we want them done. God does things when He knows they should be done. Why did God delay sending the Spirit? We could speculate on that question, but really we do not know. We do know God sent the Spirit when He knew it was the right time. We must remember, "And let us not be weary in well doing: for in due season we shall reap, if we faint not" (Galatians 6:9).

As a result of the coming of the Holy Spirit, several things happened to these people. First, *they became of one heart and one soul.* They became an unbroken fellowship. When the Holy Spirit comes into a human heart, there is no room for hate, resentment, prejudice, or anger.

In the second place, *they had all things in common.* They simply put God and His interest above all of their material possessions. I have never believed that being a Christian means that you go sell everything you have and bring it to place on the altar of the Lord. I have always believed that being a Christian means that you would be willing to do it if you thought God wanted you to do it.

In the third place, *they spoke the word with boldness.* They became unashamed witnesses of the Lord. I once heard a man who was totally deaf explaining why he attended church every Sunday. He said, "It is true I cannot hear anything that is going on in the service. But I go to let people know whose side I am on." When the Spirit of God has come into the human life, we never hesitate to let people know we are on God's side.

A beautiful result of the coming of the Holy Spirit is described in these words, ". . . great grace was upon them all" (Acts 4:33). By *grace,* here is meant beauty, loveliness, winsomeness, attractiveness.

The final result of the coming of the Spirit was that *they attracted other followers.* We read, ". . . And the LORD added to the church daily . . ." (Acts 2:47) The Spirit-filled church is a growing church. A Spirit-filled Christian is an evangelist. People are attracted to Christ by the lives of those who profess Him.

Let me urge every person who claims to have been baptized by the Holy Spirit to read and ponder Galatians 5:- 22,23. These verses say this: "The fruit of the Spirit is love, joy, peace, longsuffering, gentleness, goodness, faith, Meekness, temperance. . . ."

Take just a miniature look at each one of these. If the Spirit of God is in your heart, you have *love* for other people. You have love for every person. You do not have to like everybody, but with God's Spirit within you, you are compelled to love everybody.

The Christian does experience sorrow—disappointment— pain—frustration—loneliness. But, when a person is filled with the Spirit of God, that person has a *joy* and overcomes all of these other emotions.

Peace. This does not mean indifference to the world. One can spend a lifetime on a desert island and still not have peace. Peace overcomes all of its enemies. It means, to use Rabbi Joshua Liebman's phrase "peace of mind." It also means peace between me and my fellowman. When I love somebody, I am at peace with that person within my heart. But, more importantly, it means peace with God.

Longsuffering. Some translations use the word *patience.* But, I like longsuffering better. It says to me that the dedicated Christian is still subject to the suffering of this world. Suffering is not a sign of God's disfavor. The Holy Spirit gives the power to bear with patience whatever hurts life may bring. Patience can live today while it waits for the morrow. I have seen Christians who have suffered a long time.

Gentleness is another one of the fruits of the Spirit. Or, as other translations say, *kindness.* We sometimes confuse kindness with spinelessness. The words are not associated at all. A person can be kind and gentle—yet, strong and powerful. The Spirit of God softens harshness in people.

Goodness. Real goodness is a trait of character which only comes through the indwelling Spirit. It is not to be confused with good deeds—rather, good deeds come as a result of goodness.

Faith. The Christian is one who believes something and knows what he or she believes. Beyond that, faith means that one would die rather than surrender those beliefs. The Christian is never unfaithful.

Another fruit of the Spirit is *meekness.* I shall never forget the first time I saw a giant Sequoia tree. I stood by that great tree and looked at its massive trunk. I thought about how deeply its roots go into the ground. I looked up and saw its magnificent height. Even though I stood as straight and as tall as I could, I felt small by the side of that great tree. I have stood by the side of great people. It has been my privilege to preach Sunday after Sunday and look into the faces of people who I feel have really achieved greatness in their lives. When one stands beside greatness, it is not difficult to experience genuine meekness. When the Spirit of God comes into our lives, we cease to become self-centered and become *God-*

centered. Pride comes from looking only at ourselves. Meekness comes through looking at God. It comes naturally to the Spirit-filled life.

The last fruit of the Spirit, which is mentioned is *temperance*. The Revised Standard Version translates it *self-control*. Really, I think that is the better translation. The Spirit-filled life is one under control.

Throughout my ministry I can honestly say that my daily prayer has been that the Spirit of God be with me. I know many times I have fallen far short. That awareness is very painful to me, but it is not the Spirit's fault. It is my fault. I continue to pray that God's Spirit will completely possess my life.

6
I Believe in Prayer

BELIEF IN PRAYER came normally and naturally for me as a child, even before I can remember. My father was a very devout minister. He served small towns in northern Georgia all of his years. There were eight children born to my mother and father. One little girl went to heaven before I was born, but the rest of us all grew up together. I was number six in the family. In these little towns there wasn't anything to do at night, and there wasn't any place to go. Back in those years we did not even have a radio. But every night after supper, we would hurry and get our school lessons done, and then we would sit around the fire and my mother would read to us. She was a good reader and more entertaining than any radio or television I ever heard or saw. I remember she read the *Miss Minerva* books. John Wilkes Booth, Lincoln, and William Green Hill became our good friends. She read us the

Uncle Remus stories. Frequently I fly across the Mississippi
River and I think about Tom Sawyer and Huckleberry Finn
and their escapades up and down that river as told by Mark
Twain. We enjoyed those books. She read us many of the
classics like *Rob Roy, Tom Brown's School Days, The Heart
of Midlothian, The House of Seven Gables, Ivanhoe, David
Copperfield,* and I could name many others. I remember how
we used to cry when Little Nell died in the *Old Curiosity
Shop.* I remember how afraid we'd be to go to bed after we
had been reading *Treasure Island.* One of the magazines I
am sure not many remember today—but it was a great experience for us—was *The Youth's Companion.* I particularly
remember the Old Squire stories about farm life in Maine. I
wish we had kept some copies of *The Youth's Companion.*

Finally bedtime would come and Papa would take down
the Bible and he would read a chapter. It really was an
interesting experience to hear him read it. He read with
feeling and with understanding, and he would comment as
he went along. Hearing him read the Bible was not a chore.
But then we would all get on our knees and Papa would pray.
I just do not have words here to describe those prayers. He
would pray about a number of things, but eventually, he
would pray about the children. He would always start with
Grace—she was the oldest. For many years Grace has lived
in New York. I saw her recently and I asked her how old she
is now, because I had forgotten. She replied, "I am forty-
odd." (Of course, she doesn't count the even years!) He
would then pray for Blanche, and for Stanley, and for
Frances, for me, and for John, and for Sarah. As long as I
will live, I will hear Papa say, "Lord, bless Charles. May he
be a good boy."

As a child, I became firmly convinced that prayer is important, and prayer is real, and prayer makes a difference.

And through all these years, I have never had reason to change that opinion.

Papa would always close with the Lord's Prayer and we would all join in and we would pray it together. Those words became very familiar to me.

I never shall forget one night when a young man, about twenty years old, came to my home and said to me that he wanted to pray, but that he had never prayed in his life. He asked me how to pray. I sat down with him and I said to him, "You know the disciples of Jesus once asked Him that same question. They said, 'Lord, teach us to pray.' " (*See* Luke 11:1.)

You know, come to think about it, that's the only thing they ever asked Him to teach them. He was a tremendous preacher. The common people heard Him gladly. But the disciples never said, "Lord, teach us to preach." Jesus performed mighty miracles. The winds and the waves obeyed His voice. He healed the sick; He even raised the dead. But they never asked Him, "Lord, teach us to perform miracles."

He told them to go out and win the world. But they never said, "Lord, teach us how to build churches."

In response to their requests to teach them to pray, He did not preach them a sermon on prayer, nor did He give them a lecture on the techniques of talking to God. Instead, He simply said, "Pray this."

I said to this young man who had never prayed before, "You take this Bible that I am giving you, and I am marking the Lord's Prayer, and you just kneel down and you pray these words, and I assure you, you will learn how to pray." I could assure him of that because it happened to me. Night after night, as I was growing up, I would kneel and I would pray with my father and my mother, and my brothers and sisters those wonderful words:

Our Father, which art in heaven, hallowed by Thy name.
Thy kingdom come, thy will be done, in earth, as it is
heaven.

Give us this day our daily bread. And forgive us our
trespasses as we forgive those who trespass against us. And
lead us not into temptation, but deliver us from evil; for
Thine is the kingdom, and the power, and the glory, forever.
Amen.

From the time I can first remember until today, I doubt
if there has ever been a day when I have not prayed those
words. Let's look at them, rather briefly.

Our Father. That is where prayer ought always to begin.
That is, prayer begins with God. So many times we begin our
prayers with our own needs, our own desires, and our own
interests. The highest purpose of prayer is to turn our attention toward God, to get God into our minds and into our
thinking.

Which art in heaven. This phrase does not locate God, but
rather, describes God. "The Old Rugged Cross" is probably
one of our most beloved hymns. In it we sing, "Then He'll
call me someday to that home far away." We have the idea
that God is way out yonder somewhere, but that is wrong.
God is as near to you as the air you breathe. Heaven is
synonymous to perfection. Really, the Lord's Prayer might
begin this way: "Our Perfect Father."

Father signifies authority. I grew up with the realization
that the one in control and in charge of our home was my
father. And, I grew up with the idea that the one in control
and in charge of my world was my Heavenly Father. He
makes the laws by which we live. But He also is our best
friend. He loves us, and is always willing to help us. There
is more said in the Bible about the providence of God than
is said about any other subject.

Notice that the prayer begins with the word *Our*. That means an inclusive love. I think it was very significant in my life that I learned this prayer as I knelt in a room with my brothers and my sisters. I realize that as I prayed for myself I was also praying for them. I have always loved Ernest Crosby's poem "The Search," in which he says:

No one could tell me where my soul might be;
I sought for God, but God eluded me;
I sought my brother out and found all three.

Hallowed be Thy name. We generally think of the word *hallow* to mean respect and reverence. It does mean that, but in this particular prayer, that really is not the meaning. We do respect God. We do have reverence for God. But, notice, Jesus does not tell us to hallow God's name; rather, the prayer is asking God to hallow His own name. If you study this petition it really means, "O Lord, reveal Thyself to me." In Bible times to know a person's name was to know the person. There are many ways in which God reveals Himself in His marvelous Creation. Truly: "The heavens declare the glory of God; and the firmament sheweth his handywork" (Psalms 19:1).

God reveals Himself through people. We read the Bible and we see the experiences of God's servants there. We see God in people all about us. Certainly the supreme revelation is through His Son, Jesus Christ.

God reveals Himself in many other ways, but especially do I like to mention the ". . . still, small voice" (1 Kings 19:12). There are times when we feel His hand upon our hand. "Hallowed be Thy name" could also read, "Make us sure of Thee, O God, that we may we understand Thee more fully."

Thy kingdom come teaches us to believe that heaven can come on earth. I will deal with this a little further later, but this is an optimistic faith. It is not a prayer for pessimistic defeatists.

Thy will be done in earth, as it is in heaven. To me this petition has always meant putting my life in God's hands. Many times we are prone to come to God and pray, "Lord, this is what I have decided and I hope You will approve." But here we see that prayer is coming to God and opening our minds and saying, "God, reveal to me what You want done." I have had many people tell me that they would do God's will if they knew what God's will was. Through countless hours of counseling, I have tried many times to explain patiently to people that maybe God has already revealed His will for them. The trouble is, they are looking too far ahead. Over and over, I have said to people, "What do you believe God wants you to do this very day?" Invariably they can answer that, but the problem is they are looking a year, or two years, or ten years ahead. I have walked down a dark road with a lantern. A lantern only shines one step ahead, but as you take that step the light moves up. Many times God reveals His will to us one step at a time, as you take that step then you see the next one.

How does God reveal His will to us? I have never heard God speak audibly. But I am confident that God *does* communicate with us. One way He reveals His will is through common sense. God gave each of us a mind with the ability to think and reason. Most of the time if we will just use the mental powers we have, we can know what is the right and best thing to do. Another way God reveals His will is through the advice of others. I feel many times some wise minister has guided me when I needed more light. I have gone to physicians, to lawyers, to accountants; I have gone to friends who had understanding. God does not give all knowledge to one person. We help each other.

Oftentimes God guides us through circumstances. So much of one's life is determined by circumstances over which he or she has no control. How do we know that God did not arrange those circumstances? Of course, as I have mentioned before, I believe that God guides us through what we call *the inner light.* Oftentimes God's guidance is unrecognized and even unsuspected. Most of us can look back and see times in our lives when we were providentially led. God does answer that prayer "Thy will be done."

But this is a dangerous prayer to pray. *Thy will be done* is really an enlistment for action! When I ask "God's will to be done on earth," I am committing my life in His service.

Give us this day our daily bread. Recently, I heard a very devout person, whom I have loved and respected across the years, make the statement "I do not believe in praying for physical things." I just simply say I *do* believe in praying for physical things. Bread is physical, and bread is representative of all the physical necessities of life—a house in which to live, clothes to wear, a car to drive, and on and on. I do not believe that physical things are bad. God made this world and it's physical and it's good, and God does not object to my having some of the physical things of life. I pray often for physical blessings, and I am thankful to God that He has answered my prayers as bountifully as He has.

Forgive us. We are conscious of our sins. The truth is, most of the time I pray I have a temptation to spend my whole prayer at this point. I have fallen short in so many ways. I have said things I should not have said; I have done things I should not have done. God knows I am repentant. God knows I want my sins wiped away. I cannot forgive my sins; I cannot correct; I cannot blot them out. My only hope is the mercy of God.

I refer frequently to my father. He was truly the best man

I have ever known. He died a lingering death with cancer.
Many nights during those last two or three months, I sat up
with him. I remember late one night he brought up the
question "What is the greatest word in the English language?" We talked about it for a time and named different
words. Finally he said, "The greatest word in the English
language is the word *forgiveness.*" He knew that his death
was not far away. That's what he had on his mind. That
made a deep impression on me. If at that time my father felt
that his greatest need was forgiveness, truly how much
greater is it *my* greatest need.

And lead us not into temptation, but deliver us from evil.
Our Lord gives us three prayers to pray for ourselves. One
is for the present: "Give us this day our daily bread." One
looks both to the past and to the present: "Forgive us our
sins." The third prayer looks to the future. But we feel less
need of this than any other prayer. We know we need bread;
we know we need forgiveness; but we are not afraid of temptation. What do we feel when we look to the future? We fear
poverty; we fear sickness; we fear pain; we fear defeat.

But we feel that we can handle the temptation and evil that
comes our way. The truth is, however, many times some
tragedy or sorrow brings out strengths that we did not realize
we had. On the other hand, it often happens that temptation
brings out weaknesses that we did not know we had. Jesus
felt that we needed to pray about our temptations. One of the
most sublime verses in all the Bible is in the little book of
Jude: "Now unto him that is able to keep you from falling,
and to present you faultless before the presence of his glory
with exceeding joy" (verse 24). That is a beautiful thought,
that no matter what may come our way, God is able to keep
me from falling. The biggest lie of the devil is that we have
to sin. "After all, we are human," we say. Somehow, in

saying that, we pull down many of our standards and our highest resolves. We do not *have* to sin. With God's help, we can face any temptation and overcome it.

The other night I went to a concert presented by a great symphony orchestra. One of the numbers closed with a mighty crescendo of crashing cymbals and loud drums. It was a thrilling moment, and I think that's the close of the Lord's Prayer. It truly is a mighty, glorious, thrilling statement: "For Thine is the kingdom, and the power, and the glory, forever. *Amen.*" Here is confidence in complete victory by God in our own lives and in our world.

One of my most memorable experiences in prayer came at the altar of Grace United Methodist Church in Atlanta, on the Saturday afternoon before I was to preach my first sermon there as pastor the next morning. I grew up in small towns in northern Georgia where my father was the pastor. I was born in Newborn. There is a story that Newborn originally was named Sandtown, but an evangelist came there once and had a great revival meeting in which everybody in town got converted. As a result of that revival, they changed the name to *Newborn.* The names of the other towns where I lived do not mean much to people who are not familiar to that part of Georgia. But I like to remember every one of those towns: Washington, Winterville, Bowman, Tate, Cornelia, Bowden, Chipley, which is now named Pine Mountain. Each one of those towns has a special meaning and significance for me. To this day, there are people in every one of them that I still love.

When I started my ministry I began in Whitesburg, which at that time had a population of 215 people. While I was a student at Emory University, I served one year at Sylvan Hills Church in Atlanta, which is now Mary Brannon. Then I went to Blue Ridge, Acworth, Douglasville, Thomson. No

minister could have been happier than I was in those towns.
And no minister could have been supported more fully and
loved more completely. To each one of them I shall remain
indebted all of my life.

Then came my appointment to Grace Church in Atlanta.
We moved on Friday. On Saturday afternoon I went up to
look at the church. I had never been inside that church
before. I shall never forget my feelings that afternoon. It was
the *biggest* church I'd ever seen. I felt completely overwhelmed. I had never lived in a city. I knew nothing about
city people, and as I stood in that church, I would have given
all I had to have moved to some town where I knew how to
get along. I felt totally inadequate. Then it was I walked
down the aisle and knelt at the altar of that church. I had
always loved the church and been in the church, but that
Saturday afternoon, I feel I put something on the altar that
I had never put there before. I prayed for God's strength and
guidance. Kneeling there that Saturday, a peace and an assurance came into my heart. Suddenly, I was not afraid any
more. I remained as pastor of Grace Church for twelve years
and during those years I worked hard, but I never was afraid
again. On Sunday morning, the church was filled to capacity,
and it was a wonderful service. I asked the people to come
back that night, and they did come back. In fact, the church
was packed—with chairs in the aisles. At the close of my
sermon, I told them about my experience of praying at the
altar on Saturday afternoon before. And I suggested that any
who felt the need—as the organ softly played—come and
kneel and pray. The people lined up in the aisles to pray. I
repeated that invitation every Sunday night as long as I was
pastor there. During those twelve years, we averaged more
than a thousand people every Sunday night. And, half of
them would come and kneel and pray at the altar. I could
write a dozen books telling the experiences that people had

in the altar service. I saw that church grow from twelve hundred members to become the largest Methodist church in the Southeast. The growth came as a result of the people that prayed at the altar.

As I think back over my life, there is one experience that I remember vividly that has helped me in this matter of prayer. When I was a little boy, there was a junkman in the community. He had a horse and a wagon and would go around the town gathering junk from the various houses. I had made friends with him, and he would let me sit up by his side and drive the horse. I enjoyed that and I liked him —so much so, that I said to my father I did not want to go to school any more; instead I wanted to work with the junk-man and I wanted to be a junkman when I grew up. I was making a sincere request. I really meant that, but my father was wiser than I. He could see further than I could see and my father very kindly said, "No, you can't be a junkman; you must stay in school." That is a simple little experience, but I have remembered and profited by it across the years. When we pray sometimes God says *yes.* Sometimes God says, "WAIT." But, sometimes God says *no.* As Tagore expressed it, "Thou didst save me by Thy hard refusals." Today, as I look back over many years, I really think I am as happy over some of God's refusals to my prayers as I am over some of His granting of my prayers.

Across the years, one of the things I have taken most seriously is the request of people to pray for them. I have believed for a long time that one of the uses that God has for me is to pray for other people. More than half of my mail is requests for prayers. I answer every one of those letters assuring the writer that I am praying. When I pray for another person, I do four specific things.

First, *I pray definitely for that one person I name.* Second, *as I hold that particular person in mind, I think of God.* It is very important to have the person and God together in the mind of the one praying. Third, *I think of my prayer as lifting that person into the presence of God.* I remember that Augustine said, "Without God, we cannot; without us, God will not." I think of myself as supplying human cooperation that is necessary to bring a person and God together. And fourth, *I seek to pray positively.* I do not dwell on the person's weakness, or sickness, or wrong. Rather, do I picture in my mind the answer that I feel is best.

Across these many years, it has been a thrilling experience to have many letters from people saying that prayers have been answered. I do know it makes a difference when we pray.

I would like to write more pages about prayer, because really it is the main emphasis of my ministry. I have written three books on prayer—*All Things Are Possible Through Prayer, Prayer Changes Things,* and *The Lord's Prayer.* These all express my belief and feelings about prayer.

7
I Believe in the Kingdom of God on Earth

NOW I AM ABOUT to enter into an area where I feel sure some will disagree with me. But remember, the important thing is not whether or not you agree or disagree with me. The important thing is *that you know what you believe.* Many of the most valuable books in my study contain statements that I violently disagree with. Across the years, I have deliberately sought out authors that stimulate my thinking and with whom I can argue. They are the ones I like the best. I never get angry with an author that makes a statement that

I am in disagreement with. He forces me to sharpen my own beliefs so that I can answer him.

Anyway, here is an area of controversy. Many nights I listen to a radio station in Del Rio, Texas, as I am returning in my car from some engagement. This station has a number of preachers and I enjoy hearing what they say. I shall never forget one night that I tuned in and a man was fervently preaching. As I listened to him, I felt that he was completely sincere. I had no doubt but that he believed every word he was saying, but I did not believe one word he was saying. He was talking about the signs of the times, and how the world was getting worse, that the end of the world is near.

I just do not believe that. I do not think the world is getting worse. I think the world is better today than it was yesterday, and I think it will be better tomorrow than it is today. As I write these words, there are some people gathered together in a town in Arkansas waiting for the end of the world. In my opinion, they will wait a long, long time.

Not long ago, along the roadside somebody put in a concrete post and on it these words: JESUS IS SOON COMING. The thought occurred to me that if He is coming so soon, why did they use a concrete post? It looks like a wooden post would have been sufficient.

I believe that God is stronger than Satan—that love is stronger than hate—that goodness is stronger than evil—that righteousness is stronger than sin. I do not believe that God is going to be defeated in His world.

One of the popular sports of certain people is to depreciate the young people of this day and this generation. The truth of the matter is that has been the case for a long time. Go back and read the writings of Plato and you will find that he said that the young people of his day were going to the dogs. Every generation since has said the same thing.

But it is simply not the truth.

I always enjoy preaching on the campus of some college or university. Last year, I was at a university for four days. I stayed in the boys' dormitory. Now that is an experience in itself! It seemed to me that those boys never slept. All night long I could hear coming and going. But during those four days with them, I watched them and I studied them, and I was delighted with what I saw. To begin with, the young people today have stronger physical bodies than their parents; they have better food, and they know better how to take care of themselves. All the athletic records of a generation ago have been broken. The human race is growing stronger and healthier.

In the second place, young people today know more than their parents knew a generation ago. The average high-school graduate today is better educated than a college graduate was thirty-five years ago. This was proven to me in a very embarrassing manner. My wife and I have three children whom we appreciate very much. They are wonderful and delightful, and we love them dearly. When our oldest son, Charles, Jr., was entering the university, he was to take an entrance exam. I decided I would take the exam with him. After all, I had had quite a few years in college and seminary, and naturally knew more than he knew. (And this is as good a place as any to say that I own a Phi Beta Kappa key, which for years my wife has worn as a charm on her bracelet.) To make a long story short, the reports came back he had out-scored me twelve points on that exam. From then on, when he informed me that he knew more than I knew, I just had to bow my head and admit that he did.

Most parents today could not pass an entrance exam to most universities. Our young people are smart and they do know more. It's harder today to graduate from college than it was a generation ago.

More importantly, young people today have higher ideals and better principles than their parents and grandparents had. I know to some it sounds like heresy, but sit in a bull session on the campus of a university as I have done many times, and listen to these students talk about the world they want to build. It will thrill your heart.

One of my most thrilling experiences is to visit one of our church seminaries. Those young men and women there preparing for the ministry are intelligent and dedicated. I have no doubt that in years to come the church will be in better hands than it is today.

Anybody who thinks the world is getting worse has not read history. The world never has been perfect, but we are making a lot of progress and we have come a long way.

Our Lord taught us to pray, "Thy kingdom come." Surely, He believed not only in the possibility but in the actual fact that it would come. One night Jesus locked the door of that little carpenter's shop for the last time. He must be about His "Father's business." That business was to bring God's kingdom on earth. The text of his very first sermon was ". . . the kingdom of heaven is at hand" (Matthew 4:17). That was the one theme of His preaching all the way. He never lost His faith, and even on the Resurrection side of His grave, He talked to His disciples of the kingdom of God. (*See* Acts 1:3.)

As we pray this petition in the Lord's Prayer, it is well to underline that word *come.* It is so much easier to pray, "Thy kingdom go." It is much easier to pray for conversion of Africa than it is to face honestly to the sins of our own lives. It is easier to crusade piously for world peace than it is to forgive a neighbor who has done us wrong.

Across the years it has been my privilege to preach to

many people. I am now in my sixteenth year as pastor of a church of eleven thousand members. Twice every Sunday morning I preach in the great sanctuary filled with people. In addition, every Sunday the sermon goes out over television and over radio. It's easy for me to stand up and say to people to let the kingdom of God come in their hearts. But over and over, I am reminded of David Livingstone. I have always been interested in him because I was named for him. My father was a great admirer of Livingstone, and so when I was born, he named me after his father, who was Charles, and my middle name is Livingstone. I have read many stories and books on him, and I remind myself of the fact that he wrote in his diary, "My Jesus, my King, my life, my all, I again dedicate my whole self to Thee." There is a statement from Saint Paul that literally haunts me. He said, "But I keep under my body, and bring it into subjection: lest that by any means, when I have preached to others, I myself should be a castaway" (1 Corinthians 9:27).

When I talk about the kingdom of God on earth, surely it means that I look in my own heart and plead for God's cleansing power. It means that I bow before Him in faith and obedience. I can talk about all the sins and tragedies of the world, but let me be sure that I have committed myself, and once I am fully committed, I have more confidence in God's power in this world.

I can sing with my whole heart,

> The kingdom is coming, O tell ye the story,
> God's banner exalted shall be!
> The earth shall be full of His knowledge and glory,
> As waters that cover the sea!

I believe when I line up on God's side, I am on the winning side.

8
I Believe in the Church

SINCE THIS BOOK is my spiritual autobiography, let me approach my belief in the church from my own experience. My first memory is living in Washington, Georgia. At that time my father was pastor of four rural churches. They were Smyrna, Mount Zion, Pierce's Chapel, and Bethel. In those years my father drove a horse and buggy. Not only did he have services on Sunday, but also he would have a Saturday-morning service. When I was about three years old, I began going with him to his churches. He would let me hold the reins of the horse and I felt like I was driving. It was a great experience for me. He would preach Saturday morning and then we would visit around in the community that afternoon. We would spend the night with somebody, and then he would preach on Sunday morning and usually stay over for the Sunday-night service. Then we would get home late Sunday night. I literally grew up going to church, and I thought it was a great and a glorious experience.

I remember joining the church—that experience is as clear in my mind as it was the day it happened. Papa was preaching in a revival at Smyrna. At the close of the service he said, "If there is one here who would like to give his or her life to Christ, and unite with the church, come forward and give me your hand." I was barely six years old at the time. I didn't understand what church membership meant. I could not even read the Apostles' Creed, much less explain it. But I felt like I wanted to do what my father had said, and so, even though I had not talked it over with anybody, I stepped out and started walking down the aisle. As long I live, I'll never forget what happened. My father saw me coming, and he stepped over the railing around the altar and met me in the aisle. He put his arm around me and said, "Son, I am glad you came." I had not been in any membership training class and there was a lot I didn't know, but I am glad he didn't say that I was not old enough and that I should wait until I understood all about it. I have been back to Smyrna after I became a preacher and preached in that church. That white, wooden church in Wilkes County, Georgia, has a special meaning for me.

Also, my own experience has influenced my ministry. I have always felt that children were wiser than adults sometimes gave them credit for being. When a child has said to me that he or she wanted to join the church, I have been willing to receive him or her. I think something else affected me at this point.

When I lived in Georgia, I had a very dear friend who had been a schoolmate of mine. Later he became very prominent throughout the state and also the head of a large manufacturing concern. He became very wealthy and very influential. Also, he was a great layman in the church. He taught a Sunday-school class and did other things for the church. But then he quit. I asked him one day why he had quit, and he told me why. Just the retelling of that story still bothers me very much.

One February his little son came to him and told him that he wanted to join the church the next Sunday. His father was extremely happy about it and called the minister of the church to tell him that next Sunday his son would be joining. The minister explained that they would be having a church-membership class for children before Easter, and then on Palm Sunday he would take all the children in as a class. But, my friend explained that his son wanted to join next Sunday; he didn't want to wait until Palm Sunday. But the minister said, "No, he can wait and join with the other children." He would not receive him.

Tragically it happened the very next week. That little boy fell in a pond and was drowned. My friend very bitterly said to me, "Charles, I will never enter again the church that would not accept my little son."

During the last twenty-eight years I have received more people into the Methodist church than any other Methodist minister in the world. I am now the pastor of a church of eleven thousand members. Some of my preacher friends have said that I was not strict enough about who I receive into the church. Perhaps they are right—but on the other hand, if I'm to be faulted I would rather be faulted on that side. I have opened the doors of the church as wide as I could, and I have said to people, "I want you to come. The church welcomes you; God welcomes you; and I will receive you." I have never felt that the church was a "communion of saints." I have always felt that it was a "school for sinners."

I always loved to sing:

> Let not conscience make you linger,
> Nor of fitness fondly dream;
> All the fitness He requireth
> Is to feel your need of Him.

So you see it is natural for me to believe in the church because I literally grew up in it. I was born in a house that belonged to the church. When I finished high school it was in the days of the depression. My father was making a very small salary. But there was a little church school in northern

Georgia, Young Harris College, that opened its doors and let me come. Across the years, every opportunity I ever had came from the church. Nearly every friend I ever made in my life was a result of the church. I know the church is not perfect. I know there a lot of people in the church who do not live as well as they ought to live.

My dear mother died a few years ago at the age of eighty-seven. It may be that my mother had some faults. It may be that she was not perfect. But, I do not want anybody to talk to me about the faults of my mother. I feel the same way about the church. I don't want to hear the church criticized. The church is the best thing that ever came into my life, and I not only believe in it—I love it.

Not only do I love the church, I belong to it. I can point yonder and say, "That is my car." That means it belongs to me. I can sell it. I can give it away. I can drive it any direction I want it to go. It is my car; it belongs to me. But, when I point and I say, "My church" that doesn't mean the church belongs to me. It means I belong to the church. That means I cannot do with the church what I want to do with it. On the contrary, it means the church can do with me what it wants to do with me.

When it was announced that I was moving from Grace Church in Atlanta to the First United Methodist Church in Houston, one of my preacher friends called me and asked how I felt about moving to Houston. I told him that I was very excited about it, that I felt the First United Methodist Church in Houston was the greatest Methodist pulpit in the world, and it was a thrilling and a glorious opportunity. And then he said this to me, "Charles, suppose the bishop had called you and said he was sending you to the Blairsville Circuit?" Now I have always loved Blairsville. It is located up in the lovely mountains of North Georgia, but it is certainly not one of the top appointments. I said to my friend these words, "If I had been appointed to the Blairsville Circuit, I would have gone, and I want to tell you something else, when I got there they would have had the best preacher they have ever had." That's the truth. I was being appointed to the largest church in Methodism, but I would have been willing to go to the smallest church in Methodism. I belong to the church and I will go wherever the church sends me the balance of my days.

Now, as I talk about "the church," I am not talking about the Methodist church. I happened to be a Methodist because my parents were Methodists. If my father had been a Baptist preacher, I'd be a Baptist preacher, and so on. Most of us belong to the church we belong to because of circumstance. Then later on, we learn to defend the church we belong to. I could be happy to belong to any church that names the name of Jesus Christ. I have never been a denominationalist. I do not believe in uniting all the churches in one denomination. I think it is good that we have all of the various denominations, and I do not want to change them. I can honestly say that I rejoice whenever I hear of any church that prospers. It matters not to me what denomination it is. I feel as John Wesley said, "If your heart beats with my heart, in love and loyalty to Jesus Christ, give me your hand."

As I point out above, I did not join the church because I had any reason to, I just joined because I grew up in it, and always was a part of it. But as the years have come and gone, I have developed reasons why I believe the church is important—yea, I would even say *essential.* Let me list briefly here my reasons for believing in the church:

First, *there is no such thing as a solitary religion.* Religion is both love for God and love for man. It involves both the

Fatherhood of God and the Brotherhood of Man. Robinson
Crusoe could not be a well-rounded religious man as long as
he was on that desert island by himself. The church provides
opportunity of fellowship between people. Christian people
sing sincerely "Blest be the tie that binds our hearts in Christian love."

The ministerial staff and I at the church where I am now
the pastor conduct an average of four funerals every week.
About half of these are members of the church and the other
half are people who are not members of a local church, but
have listened to us on radio and television, and the family
requests that we have the service. I have noticed over many
years that when a person is active in a local church, there will
be many more people at his or her funeral than otherwise.
That is an indication of what I am talking about.

Second, *the church is necessary to human nature.* The two
driving urges of man are self and the herd. Man has a social
instinct which is frustrated if man does not work out his
spiritual life in corporate fellowship. People like to congre-
gate with each other, and one of the businesses of the church
is to provide a place for people to be together. The church
should not only provide opportunities for worship and study,
it also needs to provide opportunities for play and fellowship.
Once some boys were walking down the street in a little rural
community. As they passed by they heard a man say, "The
young people in this town are going to the devil." One of the
boys turned around and said, "Mister, in this town there is
no place else to go." I think the church needs to provide a
place for people to go to be with each other.

Third, *the church is the extension of the Incarnation.* We
read, "And the Word was made flesh, and dwelt among
us . . ." (John 1:14). Man did not understand God until He

became incarnate. A building is the incarnation of an architect's dream. A book is the incarnation of an author's thoughts. Jesus is the incarnation of God, and the church is an extension of that incarnation, in that the church is the body of Christ. As Saint Paul put it, "Now ye are the body of Christ, and members in particular" (1 Corinthians 12:27).

Fourth, *the church is a serving institution on this earth.* Read the history of the church and you will read of service that no other institution can match. Space would not permit even a partial listing of the educational institutions, hospitals, the children's homes, and so many other serving institutions the church has built. The church preaches the doctrine of The Good Samaritan, and also practices what it preaches.

Fifth, *the church contains the best human life in the community.* I have heard all my life that a person can be good and not be a member of the church. But, I want to say that in my own experience most of the people that I have felt were good were also members of the church. There are exceptions, I know, but in general, it is true that the church produces better people.

Sixth, *the church is the unbroken fellowship in the world.* It has a fellowship that holds when all other fellowships have snapped. The Epistle to Diognetus was written at the time when the military might of the Roman Empire was falling to pieces. In it are these words, "What the soul is to the body, so the Christians are to the world—they hold the world together." One of the texts I have enjoyed preaching all through the years is the twenty-sixth verse of the tenth chapter of First Samuel. It is, "And Saul also went home to Gibeah; and there went with him a band of men, whose hearts God had touched." To my mind that is a beautiful

definition of "the church." To begin with it is a *band* of
people, not a mob or crowd. A band signifies solidarity,
singleness of purpose, and strength. The church is made up
of people whose "hearts God has touched." It is a spiritual
fellowship that transcends all other barriers this world can
offer.

Seventh, *the church gives a sense of solidarity with all the
centuries.* The Bible was written thousands of years ago, but
it is no less written for me. My father and my grandfather
were members of the church. My grandchildren are members
of the church. The church links each generation into one
unbroken chain. When I go to church I might hear about the
faith of Abraham; I may sing a hymn based on one of the
psalms. I am inspired to stand with the disciples as they see
the Master. I walk with the apostles as they go out into all
the world. In the church, the centuries all come together.

A friend of mine told me of visiting a beautiful Gothic
church building in Amsterdam. It is called *The New Church.*
He said to someone there, "When was this church built?"
The man replied that it was built in the year 1408. My friend
was astounded and he said, "Why that was eighty-four years
before Columbus discovered America, yet you call it The
New Church." The man replied, "Across the way is The Old
Church. It was built in 1300."

A lot of things have happened in the world since Colum-
bus set out on those three little ships. Those old churches in
Amsterdam are still there. They speak of the endurance of
God's work.

I like to think:

> Oh, where are kings and empires now,
> Of old that went and came?

> But, Lord, thy church is praying yet,
> A thousand years the same.

We glory in the past accomplishments of the church. We cherish our history. But the church must constantly be working today and planning for tomorrow. In the church we need to keep looking through the windshield, instead of the rear-view mirror!

Eighth, *the denomination is not the church.* When I was a boy we used to have a home on Lake Rabun in North Georgia. We loved that beautiful, lovely lake, But really, there were five lakes in that region and all of them were fed by the same river. We give our allegiance to one of the denominations, but we realize that there are many other denominations fed by the same Spirit of our Lord.

Ninth, *the church is not the kingdom of God.* The purpose of the Christian is not to build the church, but to bring the kingdom on earth. The church is the instrument to be used in God's purpose. The church gives me a practical way in which I can work to help answer the prayer "Thy kingdom come."

Tenth, *the church is the only institution on this earth that tells me about eternity.* There are other institutions that serve humanity in many ways, but only the church points me to a home beyond this life.

Across the years, I have heard many people predicting the death of the church. But really, I have not been too impressed with that. As I write these words I am in my sixteenth year as pastor of the First United Methodist Church in Houston. This church was started the year that Houston

was founded. It is the oldest church in the city. It gives me
a feeling of stability to stand in that church and realize it has
been here as long as it has. I look out every Sunday into the
faces of people who have been members of this church for
fifty years, and forty years, and thirty years. It makes me
realize that the church is not about to close up or fail.

I remember when I was boy that people often referred to
the church as "the meeting house." I remember people saying, "Next Sunday we will go to meeting." I do not hear
those terms anymore in my church, but I wish I did.

Truly the church is a meeting house—a place where people meet God. A long time ago, Job cried out, "Oh that I
knew where I might find him! . . ." (Job 23:3). But, he is not
the last one to make that cry. The church is a place to meet
God.

I close with this thought: I have been speaking about how
long the church has lasted. There is a story about a dear old
lady who was on a guided tour of Westminster Abbey in
London. The tombs of kings and the memorials to great
people of the past were pointed out to her. Finally, she raised
a question.

"Tell me," she asked somewhat nervously." "Has anyone
been saved in this church lately?"

The church has a task to perform today.

9
I Believe in Eternal Life

ONE OF THE MOST thrilling experiences of my ministry was
preaching in a service on the Isle of Patmos. I stood on a
large rock just above the cave in which Saint John wrote the
Book of Revelation. Sitting out before me were about four

hundred people. It was my privilege to give the sermon.

I turned to the twenty-first chapter of the Book of Revelation and I began reading: "And I saw a new heaven and a new earth: for the first heaven and the first earth were passed away; and there was no more sea." That last phrase took hold of me: ". . . and there was no more sea." From that spot I could look in every direction at the sea which surrounded that little island. Suddenly, I realized what John felt. The sea was his prison—the sea kept him from going where he wanted to go and doing what he wanted to do. The sea was his handicap. As he looked into the City of God, he realized the prison doors would be opened; the handicaps would be taken away; there he would have the ability and the opportunity to realize all of his hopes—to accomplish all of his dreams.

I thought of Fanny J. Crosby. From the time she was a tiny baby she was blind. She wrote many wonderful hymns, but many of us feel that maybe her best hymn was written out of this very experience. She wrote:

> Some day the silver cord will break,
> And I no more as now shall sing;
> But O, the joy when I shall wake
> Within the palace of the King!
> And I shall see Him face to face. . . .

That was her idea of heaven—the ability to see.

I remember once after a service, when I had been preaching on eternal life, a man came up and spoke to me who had no arms. Both of his arms had been cut off in an accident. He said, "When I get to heaven, will I have some arms?" That's what it meant to him.

I think of our dear black friends in the days of slavery. They would cook the dinner and wait on the table and stand

back for other people to eat. I can understand something of
how they felt. When I was a little boy going around with my
father to his churches, on Sundays people would invite us
home to dinner. They would always have more people than
could eat at the first table, so the children would have to wait.
It seemed so long and when we finally did get to eat, there
was nothing left of the chicken but the wings and the backs
and pieces nobody else wanted. So I can understand those
dear people in the long ago who had to wait. As they
dreamed of the City of God, they sang, "I'm going to eat at
the welcome table some of these days."

Once I was preaching at the school in Talladega, Alabama.
At that time (and probably still is today), it was the largest
school in the world for blind and deaf children. I preached
there for several days in a large auditorium filled with children from kindergarten through high school. All on one side
of the building were blind, they could not see me. Those on
the other side were deaf. A teacher would stand and interpret
with her hands as I would speak.

There on the grounds was a little cottage. The first morning I was there, I went over to this cottage. At that time there
were five children there who could neither hear, nor see, nor
speak. As I went in, there was a little boy sitting just inside
the door on the floor. They told me he was five years old, but
he was little and frail for his age. I picked him up and he put
his little arms around my neck. The entire time I was there,
he held on just as tightly as he could. Finally, it was time for
me to go and I had to take his little hands and pull them away
and sit him down. He cried. It was the most pitiful crying
I ever heard. The remainder of the days that I was there,
every morning after breakfast, I would go over to that cottage and get that little boy. I would pick him up and he
would put his arms around my neck. I would walk with him

for a time around the campus.

Gradually, he put his arms around my heart, and I began to feel some bitterness and resentment toward God. I found myself saying, "God, You are not fair. You are not just. You are not loving. This little boy has done nothing wrong. He does not deserve this, but You let him be born so that he could not hear, or see, or speak." I really had some deep feeling.

Then it seemed the Lord patted me on the shoulder and said, "Now, Charles, just settle down. This is not the entire story. There will come a day when I will open his little eyes, unstop his ears, and loose his tongue."

What is your dream? What is your bitterest disappointment? Tell me what it is and I can tell you what heaven means to you.

One of the most thrilling experiences I ever had was during a Thanksgiving service at Grace Church in Atlanta while I was pastor there. The church was filled with people and we were singing:

> Come, ye thankful people, come—
> Raise the song of harvest home.

As we sang, I happened to notice a couple sitting on the second seat. They had one son; he was a wonderful boy. He had graduated from Georgia Tech and was going into the army for two years. The night before he was to leave, the three of them attended church together. I saw them kneel at the altar with this boy between his mother and father. I did not hear the prayers of that father and mother, but I know what those prayers were. They were praying, "God, watch over our boy and bring him back home safely." He went to Korea and he had only been there a few months when the message came that their son had been killed in action. They were singing, "Come, ye thankful people, come."

I looked a little farther back and I saw a lady I had known for some years, her hair now streaked with gray. I knew that her greatest desire was to be married and have a home, and have children. At the time when she could have married, both her father and mother were invalids. There was nothing else for her to do but stay at home and care for them. Her father died eight years later; her mother died twelve years later. Now her chance was gone. She lived in an apartment alone. But she was singing, "Come, ye thankful people, come."

I saw this one and I saw that one, but away back in the corner was a man I especially saw. He was a man about thirty-five years old. His record was such that he would get in jail and get out—then get in again and get out. Every time he got out of jail he would come to my office to see me. He would usually get there just before lunchtime. There was a little restaurant down the street and I would say to him, "Let's go down and eat lunch and we can talk there." He was always ready to go, and we became real good friends. Gradually, he told me his story. As a little boy he lived on one of the sorriest, poorest streets in Atlanta. He did not remember his mother. He and his father lived alone together. He told me how they didn't have any cooking utensils. His father would open a can of beans or something, and heat it on a gas jet and they would eat out of the can. The only place he had to play was that dirty street. Nobody ever kissed him goodnight, or tucked him into bed. Nobody ever taught him to say his prayers before he went to bed. That was the chance that he had. But—there he was that day singing, "Come, ye thankful people, come."

As I saw so many people, suddenly I said to myself,

"Thank God, for the Judgment Day!" Until that moment I had always been afraid of the Judgment Day. I dreaded the time when God would open the book to the page on which my name was written and read all the things I had done wrong and judge me. But that day I realized that isn't what it's all about. There is going to come a day when the wrongs of life will be righted.

What is your greatest disappointment? I tell you mine. I do not remember the day when I did not expect to be a preacher. As a little boy, I would slip into my father's church during the week and stand in a chair behind the pulpit and preach to the empty church. When I was nineteen years old I was appointed as a pastor of three little churches. Across these years, I have never been anything but a preacher. God has given me many opportunities to preach. I have been the pastor of wonderful churches where large numbers of people attended. I have preached in forty-nine of our fifty states. (The one state I have missed is Alaska, and I hope to go there sometime.) I suppose I have averaged preaching more than one sermon a day during my entire ministry. But here is my problem: I have never concluded a sermon without a feeling of disappointment. I read books; I work on my sermons, but —somehow—I never can feel that I have said what I was trying to say.

I am like the little boy the teacher asked, "What is a vacuum?" He replied, "Teacher, I've got it in my head, but I just can't say it."

Every time I stand up to preach I feel like I have it in my heart—but somehow—I just can't say it. And I tell you it really is a heavy burden. You ask me what heaven is? For me, heaven is a chance to preach and when I have finished I will have said it just like it ought to be said. What a wonderful experience that would be!

As he looked into the City of God, John said, "And there was no more sea."

When I think of eternal life, I think of the words of our Lord to the man who was dying by his side. To him he said, ". . . To day shalt thou be with me in paradise" (Luke 23:43). Notice those pronouns: *thou . . . me.* He was saying that they would be together and would know each other. Before I was born my father and mother had a little girl named Ruth who died. Other children came into the home, but they always kept Ruth's picture in a little gold frame on the mantelpiece. More than once I have seen my mother or my father looking at that picture and wiping away a tear. When my father entered the City of God, I know he did not care whether they had a gate of pearl or of oak. It made no difference to him whether the streets were paved with gold or with concrete. He wanted to see little Ruth. If she had not been there, or if he had not known her, then even heaven in all its glory to him would have been a disappointing place.

I know this brings up some problems. But somehow, I also know that all of those problems are solved in heaven. I don't worry about the problems of the next life.

We remember how at the grave of Lazarus, Jesus said, ". . . Lazarus, come forth" (John 11:43). He was Lazarus on this side; he was still Lazarus on the other side. Jesus said to Martha, ". . . Thy brother shall rise again" (v. 23). He was her brother on this side—he was still her brother on the other side. The Greek language has no word for our word *personality.* So, in translation we talk about the *resurrection* of the body, and we think in terms of the physical body. In the Apostles' Creed we say, "I believe in the resurrection of the body." But really, it is the survival of the personality. This physical body of ours goes back to dust. It is the person who survives. Seeing those we love and having fellowship with them again is a glorious expectation.

But—right at this point—I find myself oftentimes troubled. Also we will meet again those whom we have done wrong—those we have been untruthful to—those we have hurt—those to whom we have been disloyal—those to whom we have been dishonest. That is not a very comforting thought. All of us have some people we would just as soon not meet again!

In the City of God the truth will come out, and I can imagine many situations in this life in which the truth would be very painful.

On the other hand, I know that heaven is a place where all the wrongs are righted, all the sins are forgiven, and all these things in our personal relationships will somehow be straightened out and they will be all right. Thank God for that assurance and that prospect.

There are four chapters in the Bible which especially help me in my belief in eternal life. At times I like to read these four chapters at one sitting. They firm up my own faith.

The first one is John 14. Here Jesus is speaking to His closest friends about His own leaving. They were noticeably and visibly disturbed. Here He gives them three reasons why they can have faith instead of fear. First, He said, "Ye believe in God" (v. 1). What a tremendous difference that makes! It means that we are in a world that was created—it just did not happen to be here. It means there is One who can handle every situation. We are not orphans; we are not alone. We believe in God.

Second, He said, "Believe also in me" (v. 1). No one of us is good enough. But we do not face eternity trusting in our own righteousness. Everyone of us stands in need of a Saviour.

Third, He said, "I go to prepare a place for you" (v. 2).

There is a definite place where people live after death. Where that place is, exactly what it is like, what people do there, and many other questions, are not really of prime importance. The important fact is, *there is a place;* it is God's House; it is prepared; and it is available to each and every one of us through faith in Christ.

The remainder of John 14 is a beautiful, inspiring statement to give one confidence and courage.

Then I like to read John 20. Jesus had died and had been buried. His closest loved ones were both hopeless and afraid. Then came Mary Magdalene to the tomb on Sunday morning, and found the stone rolled away. She ran to tell His disciples. These disciples came and they found that the tomb was empty. But none of them thought Jesus had risen.

After the others had gone, Mary stood outside the sepulchre weeping (*see* v. 11). It was then that the Lord appeared unto her. She became sure that He was alive. That chapter also tells about how He appeared to the disciples that Sunday night, as they were trembling with fear behind closed doors. After that experience they never were afraid again. Also, the chapter tells how eight days later, He appeared again unto His disciples and how the doubt of Thomas was taken away.

In Jerusalem today, they will show two places which are claimed to be the tomb of Jesus. We are not sure which one of these is the place, but we are sure that both tombs are empty. And when I become sure of Christ's Resurrection, I have no doubt as to the fact of eternal life. There are still questions I cannot answer, but I know that He promised, ". . . because I live, ye shall live also" (John 14:19). I believe that.

The third chapter that I like to read is 1 Corinthians 15. To my mind, this chapter is the greatest statement of the Christian faith that has ever been made. (Of course, when I say that, I am not including the words of our Lord.)

Saint Paul begins, "I declare unto you the gospel. . . ." We all know that the word *Gospel* means *good news*. Many times a preacher can preach the truth and yet not be declaring the good news. For example, I may say diphtheria is a bad disease; that is true but that is not good news. The good news is that there is a vaccine that can prevent diphtheria—or a medicine that will cure diphtheria.

I may say that man is a sinner—and that is true. But that is not the good news. Or, I may say the world is bad, and I can spend every sermon I preach talking about all the bad things in the world, and I would be telling the truth. But neither would that be the good news. The Gospel is that there is One who can take a sinful person and redeem that person; or, take a bad world and make it good. *That is* the good news.

Next in this chapter Saint Paul tells us what the Gospel is. There are three main parts.

First, "Christ died for our sins" (v. 3). There are several things that one can say about that, but one thing is that He believed in something enough to die for it. I know there are people who feel that the Christian faith is not important, and they give very little time or attention to it. But, then let us remember the Son of God believed that it was important enough to die for it.

Most important, some mighty deed was accomplished that day on Calvary. Something was done that forever makes a difference in man's relationship with God and God's relationship with man. No one of us can explain it. It goes beyond human understanding, but by faith we can accept it.

The second point of the Christian Gospel Saint Paul makes is ". . . he rose again the third day . . ." (v. 4). Man had done his worst. We remember the betrayal at Gethsemane, the shameful trials, the march to Calvary, the nails being driven into His flesh, the ridicule, and His death. We know that He was buried in a tomb, and the tomb was sealed with a large stone. We know that around that tomb was placed a guard of Roman soldiers.

Then God took over. The earth began to shake; those soldiers became as dead men, an angel came and rolled away the stone, and the Lord, Jesus Christ, came walking out of that tomb into the sunshine.

I have visited the place where John Wesley, the founder of the Methodist church, is buried. But nobody can visit the place where Jesus is buried. He is not buried anywhere. He is alive.

Then the third point of the Christian Gospel is: We shall live. Saint Paul triumphantly declares, "But thanks be to God, which giveth us the victory through our Lord Jesus Christ" (v. 57). Our lives are not going to end up in a ditch in some cemetery.

The fourth chapter I like to read is Revelation 21. Saint John was exiled on the Isle of Patmos. He had been faithful and patient so long that God pulled back the curtain and let him look over into the other side. Earlier in this section I mentioned how he saw ". . . there was no more sea." In this chapter I especially like to read that fourth verse. It has a melody that thrills the human soul. Read again the words: "And God shall wipe away all tears from their eyes; and there shall be no more death, neither sorrow, nor crying, neither shall there be any more pain: for the former things are passed away."

III
What I Proclaim

10
About the Importance of Preaching

WE HAVE ALL heard the saying "A picture is worth a thousand words." I never doubted that statement until recently. I got to thinking about what you could do with a thousand words and I discovered that with far less than a thousand words one could write the Lord's Prayer, the Twenty-third Psalm, the Hippocratic Oath, a sonnet by Shakespeare, the Preamble to the Constitution, Lincoln's Gettysburg Address, and the Boy Scout Oath. I submit to you that those thousand words are worth more than any picture on this earth. Words are important, and that brings me to preaching.

Since I first entered the ministry, I have always believed that preaching was the most important thing that I did. Across these years, I have worked hard on my preaching. Saint Paul spoke of ". . . the foolishness of preaching . . ." (1 Corinthians 1:21). But, I believe it is incumbent upon every preacher to not make it more foolish than it really is.

When I was a student in the School of Theology at Emory University, I heard a story that had a profound influence on my preaching. I do not remember who the man was who told it, but he was an outstanding preacher and this is the story. He told about how that he had finished seminary and had been sent to a church as the preacher. He had worked long and hard on his sermon. He wanted to impress the people with the fact that he was an educated man. He wanted them to know that he knew the meaning of scholarship.

Finally, on Saturday morning someone knocked at his door. He met there a woman who obviously was elderly and very plainly dressed. She told him that she was a member of his church, but that she lived alone and was poor and could not contribute any money to the church. She told him that she made a living by washing clothes for other people. Because she wanted to contribute something, and because he was not married, she wanted him to know that every week she would come by and get his clothes and wash them for him.

He noticed that her back was stooped, that her hands were rough, and he knew that she was acquainted with hard work. But he also saw in her a beautiful spirit of love and of giving. He realized that she would not understand the sermon that he was going to preach the next morning. He worked all day rewriting that sermon with that woman in mind. He felt that nobody in church was more important than she was. Then he told us that from then on, he never wrote a sermon that he did not feel that she would understand.

That story had a lot to do with shaping my own preaching. Across these years, I have worked hard never to use a word that I did not feel every person in the congregation would understand. It is not difficult for a preacher to learn a few big words to put in his sermon. They may even impress some people that he is knowledgeable, but that's not really the purpose of preaching. When I went to Young Harris College I took Greek. There were only four students in the class and our teacher was the best teacher I ever had in college. His name was W. L. Dance. I had a deep love and affection for that man. But, he was a very hard teacher and he expected you to do the work. I knew that every day I was going to be called on in my Greek class and so I made preparation. The result was I did better in Greek than any other subject in college. I later reached the point that I could read the New Testament in Greek as well as I could in English. And there was a time when I could have written my sermons and preached them in Greek as easily as I could have done it in English. Suppose I had preached in Greek? I am sure that the people would have been impressed with my knowledge of Greek, but they would not have understood a word I said.

Sometime ago, I heard the choir in a church sing an anthem in Latin. After the service I said to the choir director, "The anthem was well done and I am sure that those who understand Latin enjoyed it." But when I hear somebody sing, I want them to sing in English. I want to know what they are singing.

I do not expect everybody to agree with everything I say. But it is my business to be sure that the people understand what I say.

One of the things I have done across the years is read a lot of books. Back in my early ministry when my salary was mighty low, more than once the Methodist Publishing House has written me, "Dear Mr. Allen: We cannot send you any more books until you have paid for the ones we have already sent you." I always felt that if I got one thought or one illustration out of a book, I was getting my money's worth.

Speaking of the importance of preaching, some time ago I was in another state and a man pointed out a shopping center to me. It is really a beautiful center. It was tastefully built; it had adequate parking space; it was on a well-travelled thoroughfare, and it looked to me that it just had everything needed for success. But he told me that shopping center went bankrupt. I was amazed and I asked him why. He said the reason was that it had no major stores. He said you cannot build a successful shopping center with just a cluster of small stores. He explained that a successful shopping center must have some of the big stores in order to succeed.

So it is in the church. The sanctuary and the worship service is the main business of the church. All of the other activities are important, but they center around the main thing. The church that succeeds is a church with a strong pulpit and a great worship service. It is my business as the preacher to make my Sunday-morning service the greatest event I can possibly make it. It is important for me to visit the sick, to counsel, to take a part in community activities, and do all the other things that a preacher does. But let the preacher put the first thing first.

I was preaching a few days in a wonderful church in another city. I realized the people were not happy with the pastor. I thought he was a delightful man, well trained, and he gave me every impression of being consecrated to his work and to the Lord. But I knew there was a problem, and I asked one of the laymen about it. He explained that they liked the preacher, but on Sunday, when they went to church, his sermons were so poor that it was embarrassing.

I asked the preacher about his habits of study. He said to me, "Since I have been at this church, I have been so busy I have not had time to study." I did not pursue it any further, but I wondered to myself, "Busy about what?"

I have always had time to study. When we moved to Houston, we found a delightful room over the garage. We did not need the room for any other purpose, so my wife was glad to let that room be my study. It was agreed that it was my room and nobody else would come up there, or bother with it in *any* way at *any* time. If it needed cleaning up, I would clean it. We have now been here for sixteen years and the room has not needed cleaning yet—but when it does, I will do it. I spend a great deal of time in that room. I have a telephone, but I don't always answer it when it rings. I used to think that when the telephone rang, no matter what I was doing, immediately, I would have to stop and answer that phone. But I have learned now that when the phone rings, if I will just sit real still a few minutes, it will quit ringing.

The other day one of the girls in my office told me I had a long-distance phone call. Well, I was doing something else and I did not rush to answer. It bothered her a bit and I said to her, "Settle down. Nobody ever calls me long-distance wanting to do something for me."

The main thing I am seeking to say is, if a minister is to preach effectively on Sunday, he must take time to prepare before Sunday. Different preachers do it in different ways. One of the greatest preachers I ever heard in my life was Dr. George Stoves, who for many years was pastor of West End Church in Nashville, Tennessee. One day I asked Dr. Stoves how he prepared his sermons. He told me that he would think about it during the week, and then sometime Saturday he would sit quietly and think through his sermon. I asked him about his notes, and he told me that he did not make any notes at all—he just thought it out in his mind. Now, that was a method that worked for him, because, as I say, he was truly a great preacher.

Dr. Ralph W. Sockman, one of the greatest preachers America has produced, told me that he wrote most of his sermons on Saturday night after dinner. I have a friend who is a very effective preacher. He gets up at three o'clock every Sunday morning and works until eight o'clock preparing his sermon for that day.

One of the most effective American preachers of all time was Henry Ward Beecher. He would go into his study about an hour before time for the church service. He would lie there on a couch, take an envelope out of his pocket, think through his sermon, and make the notes on the back of the envelope. Truly, no man was more effective as a preacher than was Beecher in his day. I mention these just to point out that there are many ways to do it.

I have had my own method. Always on Monday morning, I put down my subject for the following Sunday. I look through my study and find all the material I can on that subject. On Monday, Tuesday, and Wednesday I read a great deal—usually, at odd hours. For example, many nights I come in at 9 o'clock after some meeting, and I can read a couple of hours until eleven o'clock. Often, I get up early in the morning and read for another couple of hours before I go to my office. I then write my sermon on Thursday. For many years, I have set aside Thursday as the day for my study. I usually go out to my study about 7:30 in the morning, and I begin writing my sermon immediately. I have had a habit of saying it out loud and then writing it down. As a result of that, my written word is the same as my spoken word. I have always written my sermons word for word. When I finish my sermon, then I am through. I never read it over. I have heard preachers talk about rewriting a sermon two, three, or four times. I have never rewritten anything. My feeling is that my first impression is usually my best impression. I try not to think about it much more on Friday or Saturday, but then Sunday morning, I will spend about thirty minutes going over my manuscript and getting it fresh in my mind. That's the way I have done it for more than forty years.

Probably, the best lesson ever given me in sermon preparation was one that I got from my father. The first summer I was a preacher, I was telling him about how difficult it was for me to get up enough to say. During our conversation I told him an illustration that I had recently read. He asked why I did not use that in my sermon next Sunday. I explained to him that I was saving that for a special occasion. I have never forgotten his reply. He said, "Son, next Sunday is the most special occasion you'll ever have. Use all you have next Sunday." I have followed that procedure. A lot of preachers have an elaborate system of filing—I have no filing system except the corner of my desk. Anything I have worth using, I put it in my next Sunday's sermon.

In recent years it has been my privilege to lecture to a large number of pastors across the nation. Many of these pastors come from very small churches. I like to tell them about receiving a letter from the minister of a church inviting me to preach. In his letter he said, "Of course, this is not a very important church." I wrote him back that his church might not be as big as some other church, but for some people his church was the most important church in all the world.

On the wall of my office is a picture of a little wooden church. It is located in White County in the mountains of North Georgia. That little church has only one room. It probably will not seat more than a hundred people—if that many. But to me, that little church is as important as Westminster Abbey, or Saint Peter's in Rome, or any other church in the entire world—because it was in that church that both my father and my mother gave their hearts to Jesus Christ. No church could be more important—as far as I am concerned—than that church is. I preach every Sunday to great crowds of people. In addition to that, my sermon goes out over television and radio. It has been estimated that I preach to 250,000 people every Sunday. But I remember that the most important statement that has ever been made on this earth was the statement that our Lord made to one person. The words in John 3:16 were spoken only to Nicodemus. It isn't the size of the congregation that determines its importance.

What I am trying to say is the proclamation of the Gospel which we call preaching, is important and it deserves the very best that a preacher can give to it. I have faithfully tried to live up to that responsibility. I guess I'll never preach a sermon that I am satisfied with. But I keep working on them in the spirit of the artist who was asked, "What is your greatest painting?" He replied, "My next one." I feel that my greatest sermon is somewhere out in front of me and I'll keep working toward that end.

II
As a Product of My Time

IN THE BOOK OF ACTS we read how the apostles were seized and locked in prison. One night an angel opened the doors. Then the angel said to the apostles, "Go, stand and speak in the temple to the people all the words of this life" (Acts 5:20).

As I look back over my years as a preacher, I feel that I have spoken "all the words." There is a tendency in every profession towards specialization. We see it in the medical profession, the legal profession, the teaching profession, and in other professions as well. But the minister of a church cannot be a specialist. He must be a "general practitioner."

Every person is, to a large extent, the product of his times. Certainly that is true with me. I was appointed the pastor of a church in 1933. That was a time of the Great Depression and I saw very clearly the effects of poverty in the lives of people. So in the very beginning of my ministry, one of the words of the Gospel that I spoke was the word dealing with the social issues of the day. People do not have an image of me as a social crusader, but the people who have heard me preach, or who have read my sermons, know that I have had a lot to say in the area of the social gospel. As a young minister, I visited rural schools where I saw children in the wintertime with nothing on but a pair of overalls and a shirt. They had no underwear, and many of them did not have a coat or a sweater. In those days, they didn't have lunches provided for them at school. They would bring their lunch from home, and many children would have, maybe a baked sweet potato for lunch—and that would be all. I knew that many of them came to school without any breakfast. In those years, I raised my voice in every possible way to the need of helping poor people get enough to eat.

I hear today that our various welfare programs are being abused. But I lived in a day when there was no welfare, no social security, and no help for the aged. It made a tremendous mark on my thinking and on my preaching. I believe and have always preached that society has a responsibility—that we are "our brother's keeper."

I hear people today complain about the power of labor unions. But there is another side to that story. I remember as a boy living in a little town where nearly everybody in town worked for one industry. There was no union, there was no protection for the worker. I remember the day that my best friend told me that his father had been fired, and they were going to have to leave town and get another job. This man had worked for this company for twenty years. Then one day a foreman got upset with him and just said, "You are fired." There was no recourse. Even as a high-school boy,

I realized the injustice and unfairness of it. And as a preacher, I have raised my voice again and again, and I have given my efforts and my time to see that the working man has some protection and a fair opportunity.

One of my problems has been racial prejudice. Though I did not realize it for many years. I grew up in a society that just accepted the fact that black people were inferior to white people. For many years I didn't question it, and I didn't ever realize that I was prejudiced. But I had an experience one night that had a profound influence on my life. I was preaching a series of sermons in the Mulberry Street Methodist Church in Macon, Georgia. Out in front of that church was lovely little park. Just at dusk, one evening I was sitting in that park thinking over the sermon that I would soon give in the church across the street. As I sat there, a black woman and her little boy came walking down the sidewalk. As they got even with the park, he turned and ran toward some swings and began swinging. His mother told him that he could not swing on those swings. He did not understand why, and he asked. She told him very firmly that those swings were for white children. As they walked out of the park that little boy looked up at his mother and said, "Mama, I wish I was a white child." Those words burned themselves into my mind and my heart. I made a vow that night that the remainder of my life I would do all I could to build the society in which that little boy could swing in the swings just like any other little boy. I have stood for the principle that all people —regardless of the color of their skin—are equal before God and should have equal opportunity.

I well remember the first black person who ever joined the church where I was pastor. It happened not long after I moved to Houston. The First United Methodist Church in Houston had never had a black member. In fact, at that time, no Methodist church in the Texas Conference had a black member. This black man came up to me after the service and said, "I want to belong to this church." Of course, I did not hesitate. I never have believed that you could put a sign WHITE PEOPLE ONLY over the door of the church of the Lord Jesus Christ. I told him we would be glad to have him, but I asked him why he wanted to join that church. I shall always cherish his reply. He told me, "I have been around and listened to a number of preachers in Houston, and I have decided that you are the best preacher in the city." Of course, I could not turn that man down. He is one of the smartest men that I have ever known! Since then, it has been my joy to receive a number of black people into the church and they have made fine members and the church is better for them. But we still have racial prejudice, and as a minister of Christ, it is my business to speak a word on that issue.

There are other issues that the church is concerned about. Alcohol, for example. There is no way of measuring the lives that are being hurt by alcohol. Alcohol may be our greatest social enemy today. I could write pages about the lives of people that I have personally counseled that are in shambles because of drinking.

Gambling is another one of the issues of our day. A few years ago, there was a vote in Texas on legalizing pari-mutuel betting at race tracks. I worked hard to defeat that issue. One of my friends came to me and with feeling asked why I was opposed to horse racing. I assured him I was not opposed to horse racing. Horse racing can be a fine sport; what I *was* opposed to was legalized gambling on horse racing. I know there are many states where gambling is legal, but I maintain it is wrong and it does great harm to multitudes of people. I would like to rid our nation of all legalized gambling.

One of the issues before us today is pornography. I know

that we have always had pornography to some extent. But today it is being beautifully packaged and sold everywhere to all ages. It cannot but do harm.

Just in recent years we have seen the rise of drugs and today it's becoming one of the great problems, even in our high schools. Surely, the preacher must grapple with this issue of drugs.

One of the stories in the Bible which I have often preached on is in the third chapter of First Kings. It's about two mothers who were claiming the same baby. They took the baby to Solomon and asked him to decide. This was before the days of blood tests and he had no real way of knowing whose baby it was. And so, he asked that a sword be brought to him and he would cut the baby in two, giving half to each. That story teaches a number of things, but one thing it teaches is the futility of the sword. If he had used the sword, the only thing that would have been accomplished was that the world would have been robbed of a life.

The year I was born (1913) a war was starting which became a world war. After it was all over, Sherwood Eddy, who was a great preacher in that day, summed it in these words, "The saddest thing is not that some ten million of our best men are dead, and the world is impoverished, victimized, embittered by hate, rent by suspicion and fear. It is that we settled nothing, made nothing safe, achieved no lasting good."

I was a preacher during World War II, and I saw much of the hurt and sorrow of that war. In those years we had flags in our churches, and we would put a star on the flag for each one of our boys and girls who went into the service. In one little country church where I was the pastor, we had only one star on our flag. I remember the Sunday that we changed that blue star into a gold star. The only boy from that little church was killed. I have visited in Japan where the cities were destroyed by our atomic bombs. I have spent some weeks in Korea and seen the aftermath of that war. I visit regularly in the great veterans' hospital in Houston. Not long ago, I received into the membership of the church a quadriplegic, who had been listening to our services on television. He is a patient in the veterans' hospital. He lost both of his arms and both of his legs in a war. I think sometimes if I could pray one prayer it would be, "Lord, let us have peace on earth."

There are many other issues, but what I am saying is, across the years of my ministry, I have faithfully tried to speak the word of social action.

In the church today, we must constantly face up to persistent racism. We must recognize more and more that women have been subordinated in the church's ministry and in our society. Nearly every city now is seeing its very core become slum areas. The church must be concerned about the housing conditions, perhaps as never before in our history. Today we need to demand more honesty and integrity among our public officials. As our population grows, we have a responsibility for the natural resources of our land. *Ecology* is a word that the church must speak more and more about. One of the tragedies of our society is our prisons. They must become institutions of rehabilitation, where the dignity of the prisoner is respected. More and more we must demand that every person in our society be given access to health care. There are so many other issues that I could spend the remainder of these pages discussing them.

I get a lot of telephone calls, but I never shall forget one. Late one night my phone rang and the man speaking was obviously upset. He asked if I were a preacher and I told him that I was. He said, "Tell the church to go to hell." Then he hung up the phone. At first I felt anger and resentment, but I have thought about that a great deal since, and I have the feeling that that man was giving the church about the best message the church could ever receive. That is the business of the church—to go where people hurt and try to bring healing and salvation.

In one of his books, Tolstoy speaks of the snares of the human soul. One of those is "the snare of society." The church is concerned with building a society which is conducive to the good life.

12
About Personal Salvation

ACROSS THE YEARS of my ministry, I have preached that we humans are sinners, and that we need to be saved from our sins. I have preached the validity of the Christian experience all the days of my ministry. I am sure that there is such a thing as a Christian experience. And here I would like to elaborate on why I know that one can be saved through faith in Jesus Christ. Let me mention several reasons:

First, I know there is such a thing as a Christian experience *because others tell us.* That is how we know much of what we know. For example, what kind of weather exists at the North Pole? I never have been there, and from my own knowledge I could not say. But others have been there and because I believe their testimony, I can say that it is cold and icy at the North Pole.

Who discovered America? I was not here, but down through the years has come the word. Today we feel confident in saying that Columbus discovered America.

They tell us that we had a war in Viet Nam. I never have been to Viet Nam. I did not see any fighting there, but because of what others have told me, I believe they had a war in Viet Nam.

I remember the revival meetings my father used to conduct. Often times he would have what he called *testimonies*. He would ask people to stand and tell what the Lord had done for them. It was impressive to me to hear one after another tell of a Christian experience and how it changed his or her life. Early in my life, I came to believe that one could experience Christ, because I had heard people tell about it.

A second reason why I am sure there is such a thing as salvation in Christ is, *because I have seen it work.* There was a day when they taught in our universities that it was impossible to build an airplane that would fly. You might have gone to one of those professors and argued until you were blue in the face, but you never would have convinced him that he was wrong. But if you could have taken him to an airfield and there—before his eyes—warmed up a plane, taxied down the runway, sailed up in the sky, circled, came back, and landed, *then*—no matter what his belief was—he would have to say, "I know an airplane is possible, because I have seen it work."

Suppose I were to lay two wires across the floor. I might say through those wires is flowing a power. However, someone might argue that since that power could not be seen, it did not exist. But suppose I attached to the end of those two wires a light bulb, and it began to shine; or an electric motor and it began to run. Then, no matter what a person may have previously believed, he or she would then know a power was flowing through those wires, because it could be seen working.

Across the years, I have seen many, many lives that I could not explain—apart from the realization that somehow

God can come into a life, and change that life, and empower that life, and save that life.

On the campus of Oxford University in England, a small band of students began a prayer meeting. From that they went out preaching on the streets and in the mines—and wherever people would listen. It started a revival that produced the Methodist church. As I look at England, and the effect that John Wesley and Charles Wesley and George Whitefield and the others had, I know that somehow they had one hand in heaven and one hand on earth—and through their lives was flowing a power. I know it because I see it work.

In my own ministry, I have seen lives changed that I could not explain apart from the power of God. Again and again, I have prayed that I might be used as an instrument for His power to reach some person who needs Him.

A third reason why I am sure there is such a thing as a Christian experience is *because it has stood the test of time.* Many things start off well, but they do not last. Many housewives have what they call their "kitchen silver." It is the silver they use every day, saving their good silver for more special occasions. To begin with, these kitchen teaspoons and forks are brighter and shinier than any sterling one might possess. But as you use it, gradually the shine is gone and it cannot be brought back. Not so with the sterling.

Some time ago, I was having dinner in a lovely home in Vicksburg, Mississippi. I commented on the silver because it was so beautiful. My hostess explained that this silver was buried during the war. (Now when you are in Vicksburg, Mississippi, and they say *the war,* you know what they are talking about!)

She explained that this silver had been buried for nearly a hundred years before it was discovered. When they found it, it was black and tarnished, but when I saw it, it was beautiful and bright. Why? It was real and genuine. It was sterling. It would last.

I am out in my car a great deal and I enjoy listening to the popular songs on the radio. But I get discouraged because by the time I learn one of these popular songs, everybody quits singing it. These songs today come in and they shine for a week or two, and then they are gone. But our great-grandfathers sang "Amazing Grace! How sweet the sound/That saved a wretch like me!" And our great-grandchildren will be singing the same song. What's the difference? One is real and genuine. It will last.

So it is with the experience of God in one's soul. We remember how Enoch walked with God, and how Abraham went out by faith. We know that Isaiah walked into the temple and saw the Lord high and lifted up, and that Jeremiah felt within him, as it were, a fire that burned his very being. We remember how the Lord said to Zacchaeus that salvation had come to his house. There was Paul on the Damascus road. We know the story of Augustine in the garden, and how Luther proclaimed that he would die by his faith. We know that Wesley's heart was strangely warmed.

Nearly everything on this earth is changed—the clothes we wear, the language we speak, the food we eat, the houses we live in, the way we travel, and so many other things. But people are still having the same experience with God today they had in Moses' day. If it was not real, it would not have lasted this long.

There is another reason why I am sure of the Christian experience, and that is *because it is so universal.* Today the Christian faith is firmly established in more than half a hundred nations of the world. There are vast differences among people today. We speak different languages, we have different

colors of our skin, our cultures are vastly different. But yet
we all experience the same Christ. The Christian faith is not
something born out of a culture. It is something beyond and
above all cultures. I have had the privilege in my trips to
Palestine to visit almost every place where Jesus visited. I
have seen His country and something of the culture out of
which He came. But I know that He is beyond and above that
limited existence. Jesus Christ transcends all social conditions and cultures of mankind.

There are other reasons why I am sure there is such a thing
as a spiritual experience. But, the main reason is, *because it
has come to me.* One of our favorite stories is in the ninth
chapter of Saint John's Gospel. It is about a man who was
blind from his birth. Jesus came by and healed him. The
Pharisees saw it and they were jealous; they claimed that
Jesus was not of God, because He broke the law of the
Sabbath Day. They asked the blind man if he really believed
that this man, Jesus, was Christ, the Son of God.

Reading between the lines, you can hear this blind man
saying that he didn't know about their Bible. He had been
blind and he couldn't read the Bible. He didn't know about
the temple because of blindness; he had not been going to the
temple. He really did not know about this man Jesus. He
certainly had never seen Him before. But, there was one
thing he *did* know: ". . . whereas I was blind, now I see"
(John 9:25).

There are vast multitudes of people who cannot explain
every detail of church history. They do not know all the
principles of theology; they are not familiar with every passage in the Bible—but who can say, "I was one thing and
Christ touched my life, and now I am something else."

Across the years, I have believed in the Christian experience.

Now that leads me to a second consideration: *How can one obtain the Christian experience?* Here is an area where there have been argument and misunderstanding. There are those who feel that there is only one doorway into a saving experience through Jesus Christ. The truth is there are many types of Christian experience one can find in the Bible. Across the years I have sought to preach to people that one experience does not necessarily have to be exactly like somebody else's experience.

Turn to the ninth chapter of the Book of Acts. There you read the experience of Saint Paul. He was journeying to Damascus, when suddenly a great light from heaven shone all around him. He fell to the earth and he heard a voice saying, ". . . Saul, Saul, why persecutist thou me?" (v. 4). In that moment, he made a complete surrender of his life. He said, "Lord, what wilt thou have me to do?" (v. 6). From that moment on he was never the same. He went into Damascus and walked down the street which was called *Straight.* I have walked down that same street and I thought about the great apostle. What a glorious experience Saint Paul had! It was dramatic, climactic, overwhelming. As long as Paul lived, he could say that on a certain day, at a certain spot, he saw the Lord.

There are many people who have had this type of an experience. Four of the happiest years of my life were spent as pastor in Thomson, Georgia. Living there at that time was one of the saintliest men I have known. We all called him Brother Brand. He had been a minister for many years and now he was retired. As the young pastor, never a week passed that I would not go and sit and visit with Brother Brand. From him I learned many wonderful lessons. Every so often I would say, "Brother Brand, tell me about when you found the Lord." (I knew the story as well as he did, but I just

wanted to hear him tell it.) His face would light up and he
would say, "Why, Charles, I can remember it as though it
were yesterday."

Then he would tell me about the old campground up in
Cherokee County and how that during camp meeting on
Tuesday morning, at the 11 o'clock service, the preacher was
preaching and he felt conviction. At the close of the service,
the preacher gave an invitation. He knelt at a tree growing
there beside the tabernacle, and he would tell me how that
kneeling there that day, the Lord saved him. He would say,
"I can take you right now and show you where the tree
stood."

When that experience happened to Brother Brand, he was
a boy twelve years old. When I knew him he was more than
seventy years old. But that experience had been the light of
his life and the joy of his heart.

There is an old song which I hear sometimes on the radio
now. It goes like this:

> I can tell you now the time; I can take you to the place;
> Where the Lord saved me, by his wonderful grace.

There are many people who can sing that song. They can
tell you the exact time and the exact place when it happened.
That is a valid experience. Now let me say that is not the only
experience; in fact, I really do not think it is the best experience.

I think Timothy had a better Christian experience than
Paul had, and I have the feeling that Paul would agree with
that. Read the first chapter of Saint Paul's Second Letter to
Timothy. He reminds Timothy that his grandmother was a
Christian, and that his mother was a Christian, and he indi-
cates that Timothy himself grew up as a Christian and never

knew anything else. If you had asked Timothy, "When did you become a Christian?" Timothy could not have given a definite answer. It did not happen at any one moment.

I remember very clearly once saying to one of our sons that I thought now was a good time for him to join the church. He immediately became very upset. It had never occurred to him that he did not belong to the church. Before that little boy was born, we prayed for him, before he could remember, we taught him to kneel and say his own prayers. Before he could walk we carried him to Sunday school. Our home was never perfect, but as best we could, we sought to have a home in which the principles of Christ dominated. He grew up with a father and a mother who believed in Christ, and who loved the church. We lived next door to the church. There was a dear old man who was the janitor of the church, and he loved that little boy. And the little boy loved that old man. Every week he would go over and help that man clean up the church and get it ready for Sunday. He took pride in working at the church. When I mentioned the thought of his joining the church, he was shocked, because not only did he think he *belonged* to the church, he felt that he was pretty much in charge of the church, and he was happy for it. That boy now is a grown man and is the president of a bank, but he still is active in the church. He loves the church, but he could not tell you when it began. Though he could not tell you when he *became* a Christian, he will say to you that he *is* a Christian.

Before I go any further, let me emphatically point out that Jesus said, ". . . Ye must be born again" (John 3:7). I believe with all my heart in the new birth. It is real and it is essential. But I am suggesting that the new birth might come so normally and so naturally that we never know exactly when it comes.

Every so often someone says to me that we do not have revivals like we used to have, and I thank God for that. I can remember when I was a boy—and even when I started out as a preacher—most of our rural churches were just one-room buildings. We didn't have much of a Sunday school and we did not pay much attention to the children and young people. But along in the latter part of the summer when the farmers had "laid by" their crops, we would have a revival meeting. I grew up in those meetings and I have conducted many of them. We would sing emotional songs, the preacher would preach an emotional sermon and then we would high-pressure children and young people to the altar of the church and into the kingdom. I can remember in my early days how that I would sing two or three hymns and I would walk out into the congregation, urging people to come and make their commitment to the Lord that night. And I saw some wonderful experience.

But, that is not the way we do it today. In our churches we have wonderful programs for children and young people. We seek to help them grow into the Christian faith.

I reject the idea that a child has to go to the devil before he comes to Christ. We do our best to keep our children from ever going to the devil in the first place.

My own personal experience is the experience of Timothy. I grew up believing myself to be a Christian and never knowing myself to be anything else.

There is a third experience that I will mention. Some time ago, a very prominent man in Houston called me and said he wanted to see me. He told me that he wanted to join the church and wanted to talk with me about it. I told him that I would come around to his office. (I have learned that many times you can know much more about a person visiting in his or her office or home better than their visiting in your office.) I sat down in his office and he told me that he was forty-four years old, but that he had not been inside of a church in more than twenty years. He had been listening to me each Sunday on the television, and had decided he wanted to join the church. But he did not know what was required of one to become a member. He told me he had already told his secretary that from then on, he wanted to send a thousand dollars a month to the church. (I was ready to take him in right then. He already was in good standing with me!) But then this man asked me to tell him how to be a Christian.

That is not so easy to do. Many times we preachers use words that sound fine but really do not mean a lot. We say for example, "Come to Jesus." Now that's a good phrase, but if a person doesn't know what it means, it doesn't help. Preachers tell people, "You need to be washed in the blood." That is a great theological truth, but I question that many people understand that phrase. I knew of an old preacher who could say "Mesopotamia" in such a beautiful way it made people cry. It didn't do them any good; it just made them cry.

Anyway, this man wanted to know how to become a Christian in language he could understand. I took my Testament and turned to the nineteenth chapter of Saint Luke. I told this man that I wanted to read him a story about another businessman who became a Christian. His name was Zacchaeus. Jesus was coming through town one day and a great crowd of people had lined the streets to see him. Zacchaeus was a man short in stature, and he could not see over the people, so he climbed up into a sycamore tree.

(Once I spent some time in Jericho looking for sycamore trees and I could only find one in the city, and it certainly was not the tree that Zacchaeus climbed.)

Anyway, Jesus saw him in that tree and stopped and told him to come down—that he wanted to go home with him for dinner. (Incidentally, I preach on this story about once a year. I point out to the people in my church that if they do not invite the preacher to eat with them, according to the Bible, he has the authority to invite himself. In that way I get a goodly number of dinner invitations.)

Jesus and Zacchaeus went to his home and then the curtain came down. They are not seen for several hours. Then the curtain went up, Jesus was heard saying, "This day is salvation come to this house . . ." (v. 9). Jesus was saying that Zacchaeus had been saved.

After reading that story I said to my friend, "What do you think happened?" He replied that he felt Zacchaeus made a simple decision. I asked if he thought Zacchaeus cried about it, or shouted about it. He replied that he did not think so; he felt it was just a quiet man-to-man decision. I asked him if he would make that same decision and he said, "That is exactly what I want to do." We knelt and prayed together there in his office, and I believe that day that man became a Christian. It was just a quiet decision.

What I am trying to suggest is, that there are many types of Christian experience. But I believe and have preached the importance of the experience in Christ as one's Saviour and Lord and Friend.

13
On My Role as a Comforter

THE PROPHET ISAIAH said, "Comfort ye, comfort ye my people, saith your God" (40:1).

One of my professors in theology school used to say rather

frequently, "Boys, in your congregation there will be broken hearts—in every sermon have a word for them." I have never forgotten that, and I have always believed that one of the words the angel would have the preacher speak is *comfort.* People can be hurt in so many ways—death takes away one we love more than we love ourselves; the prize sought in life is snatched away, and disappointment can forever remain in our hearts. The human body can be made to suffer pain. Doubt can weigh heavily on the mind.

I try never to forget that in my Bible are such words as, *Let not your heart be troubled. . . . In my Father's house are many mansions. . . . Yea, though I walk through the valley of the shadow of death, I will fear no evil: for thou art with me. . . . and God shall wipe away all tears from their eyes.*

We preachers sometimes feel that we are courageous when we sound off on some great social issue. But we need to remind ourselves constantly there are those listening to us who are having a hard time. A few Sundays ago, a couple came up to speak to me after the morning service. They introduced themselves and told me they lived in a town about fifty miles away. Then they told me that they had one son who was sixteen years old. The week before he had been killed in an automobile accident and they had buried him on Thursday. They said to me, "We just wanted to come in this morning and hear you preach." Those people needed a word of comfort.

We ministers on the staff in the church where I am the pastor conduct an average of four funerals every week. Every Sunday I stand in the pulpit and look into the faces of many, many people with whom I have been to the cemetery to bury their loved ones. My sermons every Sunday are on both television and radio. They go into many, many homes. Many of the people who listen to me are old, and can't get out very much. As one gets old in the city, there is a tendency also to be forgotten. Many of them are very lonely. They need a word, too. I preach to many people who are sick and realize their chances of living much longer are not good. That can be a frightening time. There are many young couples in a big city who are overwhelmed and need reassurance. Sooner or later, every person needs the help of the Gospel.

Not long ago a man came in to see me who had spent six years in the penitentiary. He said to me, "I just want to feel again that I belong." That man now feels ostracized and left out. He needs a special word from the minister. As I have grown older, I have found that this word has become more prominent in my preaching. I think I am no less a crusader today than I was some years ago, but I am more aware of the need of comfort in the lives of many people. I have been to the cemetery with some that I have loved the most. I know what it is to be hurt, to be disappointed, and I have learned to sympathize with a lot of people. In 430 B.C. Thucydides wrote, "It was in those who had recovered from the plague that the sick and the dying found most compassion." A preacher who has never needed comfort is not likely to be as concerned about giving comfort.

I like the story of the little girl who went to the store for her mother. She was gone a rather long time and when she got back, her mother asked why it had taken her so long. She told her mother about another little girl who had fallen and broken her doll and that she had helped her. The mother wondered what she could have done to help the little girl fix her broken doll. She replied, "I just sat down and helped her cry." Across these years I feel that I have helped a lot people cry. And I am grateful for those who at times have helped me cry.

14
About the Privilege of Stewardship

AS I LOOK BACK over my sermons, I feel that I have spoken this word *stewardship* unto the people. Across the years raising money in the church has really not been a problem of mine. I have found that people have given generously and responsibly everywhere I have served as pastor. One of the temptations a preacher faces is to let himself get frightened at the idea people will say he is preaching for money. But we need to remember that Jesus said more about stewardship than any other one subject.

As I think back across my years, there are several steward-ship experiences that stand out in my memory. One came very early. When I first started going with my father to his country churches, he drove a horse and a buggy. Well do I remember one Sunday as we were driving along the road to church, we saw an old man standing in front of his house along the side of the way. He was a retired school teacher. Everybody called him Professor Miller. In those years, school teachers made very little and I suppose they had no retirement at all. My father stopped and spoke to him. I well remember how he said to my father that he knew it was near the end of the church year and he wanted to make a contribu-tion for the church's expenses. He handed my father two one-dollar bills, saying that one was for himself, and the other was for his wife. I remember very clearly my father's saying to him that he appreciated his generosity, but that the church was in good shape and that really, they were going to pay off everything. He felt that he should keep the money.

Then Professor Miller looked up to my father, and I can hear him to this day as he said, "Brother Allen, would you deny me the privilege of giving to my Lord?"

That is the first stewardship experience of my life that I can remember, and I suspect it had more influence on me than any other stewardship experience of my life. I personally have always counted the opportunity of giving to God as a privilege, and I have never been hesitant or timid in asking other people to give.

On the mantel in the den of my home is a possession that I have had for forty years. It is a man's watch. My wife bought a little glass sphere and the watch hangs inside. It is a big, old-fashioned gold watch. In my first pastorate in Whitesburg, Georgia, there lived a dear lady named Mrs. Shannon. At that time she was probably seventy-five years old. Very faithfully she gave twenty-five cents a month to the church. Now that does not sound like much, but for her in those years, it represented a sacrifice. When she died the only thing of value she had was that gold watch, which had been her husband's before he died. She left a note saying that she wanted me to have that watch. I have kept it across the years and every time I see it, I think of that little white-haired lady. I suspect that she was one of the largest givers I have ever had in the church.

I think of another story. When I was pastor of Grace Church in Atlanta, we were enlarging the sanctuary, One Sunday, a man came up to me and gave me five ten-dollar bills. He said he wanted this to go into the building fund. Then he told me that he had been saving all the summer to get enough money to buy a new suit. At the time he gave me the money it was in September. He had saved up fifty dollars, and with that he intended to buy himself a winter suit. But instead, he gave it to me to use in the church. All that winter he came to church every Sunday wearing a thin, light-colored summer suit. In Atlanta it can get pretty cold during the wintertime, and I imagine people looked at him and wondered why a man would wear a thin suit like that in the middle of the winter. But to me he was the best-dressed man in the church. He gave his only winter suit to be used for the Lord.

When I started out as a preacher, my own salary the first year was four hundred and ten dollars. That was the total for the year. But that year I gave forty-one dollars to the church. The next year my wife and I got married and we pledged each other that we would continue our program of tithing. In those early years, sometimes it was hard. I know what it is to preach when the best pair of pants I had were patched. I didn't have money to buy any more. I know what it is for us to go a week without buying any meat because we didn't have money to buy it. I used to like strawberry jam better than anything, but I rarely ate any in those years. A jar of strawberry jam cost twenty-five cents, and you could get a jar of apple jelly the same size for ten cents. We always bought the apple jelly. I have never liked apple jelly since. I know what it is to do without things, but I can say now, that I do not know what it is to withhold my gifts from the Lord.

I have now come to conviction that I can not outgive God. God has given to me far more than I ever expected.

Here is an area where I feel it's easy for a preacher to make a mistake. Many preachers talk about how the church needs money. You don't get much money talking about your needs. More importantly, it is better to talk about how one needs *to give*. At the beginning of a church year, many churches will print a budget and send it out to all the members and go around and visit and plead with the people to give. I think that is wrong. I have not printed the budget in a church that

I have served in many, many years. People don't give because the church needs money. People give because they need to give and have a sense of stewardship.

One of the mistakes I have made across the years is that I have not asked the people for enough. In my church in Houston, we have a custom of taking up a special Christmas offering. This offering goes to various mission causes in the name of Christ. The first fourteen years that I took up that offering, it averaged about twenty-five thousand dollars a year. I went back over the record and the lowest we had any of those fourteen years was $23,000, and the highest was $27,000. Last year I did something a little differently. Instead of just asking for an offering, I wrote every family in the church asking for $100. Some did not give that much, some gave more, some gave nothing. When we counted the offering, the total was $109,000! It multiplied four times, and it happened simply because I asked for it.

I am reminded of the story of the man asking his friend how he liked their new preacher. His friend told him that he was the greatest preacher that they had ever had and then he added, "Our new preacher asked the Lord for things the old preacher didn't even know the Lord had."

I feel that people in the church will respond if they are properly challenged, and if they are asked.

One of the principles that I have held up is ". . . If ye have faith as a grain of mustard seed, ye shall say unto this mountain, Remove hence to yonder place; and it shall remove; and nothing shall be impossible unto you" (Matthew 17:20). I have again and again said to people, "If you have a problem, plant a seed."

15
About Outreach—The Main Business of the Church

HERE I COULD use the word *evangelism* or *missions*. Truly one of the basic principles of the Christian faith is that it is always reaching out for others. We never forget that our Lord said, . . . "ye shall be witnesses unto me both in Jerusalem . . . and unto the uttermost part of the earth" (Acts 1:8). I have always believed that evangelism is not the only business of the church, but it is the *main* business of the church.

It was a high experience for me one day to stand on the grave of Samuel Wesley in the same tracks where John Wesley stood and say as he said, "The world is my parish." No person can be a Christian who does not believe in reaching other people.

I guess I shouldn't boast about it, but I do feel pleased that during the past twenty-eight years (and twenty-eight years is a long time), I have received more people into the Methodist church than any other Methodist minister in the world. I realize that has happened because I have been in places where I had the opportunity. But also, it has happened because I believe deeply that winning others is my task and I work at it.

Many, many times I have preached on that beautiful story that our Lord told which begins, "What man of you, having an hundred sheep, if he lose one of them . . ." (Luke 15:4). I have often thought about that sheep that was lost.

I have never believed that the lost sheep was black and the others were white. I never believed the lost sheep hated the shepherd, or did not want to associate with the other sheep. I think the way it got lost was simply that it was out there eating grass. It was good grass and it was good for the sheep to eat the grass. I can imagine that the sheep just kept eating the grass and wandering away and finally, after a while, it looked up and it was dark. The shepherd and the other sheep were out of sight. I do not think it was a bad sheep or that it intended to get lost.

This has been pretty much my view of people. There are great numbers of people who are not angry with God; they do not hate the church; they do not resent church people. But they get interested in something—most of the time something good. It may be a business, or a home and family; it may be a ranch, or a farm outside of the city to go to on the weekends. It may be a boat. It may be a lot of things, but gradually one can get interested in something else and give to that something else all of their time and their attention. They do not take time for God; they forget about praying; they drop out of church; they become lost.

I never have felt it was my business to fuss at people who are lost. It is my business to somehow turn their attention toward God.

For many years I have told the story of the church in the little town that caught on fire. Then—as people do in little towns when there is a fire—everybody goes. All the people were standing around the church watching it burn. The preacher went around shaking hands with people. He came to one man and said, "It's good to see you; this is the first time I have seen you at church." The man replied, "Preacher, this is the first time this church has ever been on fire."

That reminds me of the time a group of young ministers came to John Wesley and asked him how he got such great crowds to hear him preach. John Wesley replied, "Young men, get on fire for Jesus Christ, and your congregation will come to see you burn."

That shepherd could have said, "All right. I have provided that sheep with a good fold in which to sleep, I have provided him with water and food and every care that a sheep can be given. If he wants to stay out in the darkness and not come in, that is his business." The shepherd could have said that —but he didn't. Instead, the story continues, ". . . doth not leave the ninety and nine in the wilderness, and go after that which is lost, until he find it?" Underscore those words *go after*. That's my business; that is the business of the church.

Let me name the name of Hoke Bell. We were classmates at Young Harris College and later in the School of Theology at Emory University. When World War II came, Hoke Bell entered as a chaplain. One day during a violent battle in North Africa, he saw one of his boys wounded on the battlefield. He asked permission to go after that boy, and the commanding officer told him that it would be very dangerous and he advised against it. But Hoke Bell was not willing to leave one of his boys on that field bleeding to death. He went out to him. He picked him up and started back, and stepped on a land mine which exploded. Both of them were blown to pieces. As I think about it, I believe that World War II did not produce a greater hero than that young chaplain, who gave his life trying to rescue a wounded boy.

One day a conductor on a passenger train was making his last run before retirement. A man asked him how he felt about his life as a conductor on a train. He replied, "It seems like I have spent my life trying to help people get home."

I don't know how many more years I have, but as I look back over my life, I feel that a major emphasis of mine has been trying to help people get home. I thank God for the opportunities He has given me.

One of the most fertile evangelistic fields of any church is its own church roll. In recent years it seems that it has become popular in churches to revise their rolls. Perhaps that is a good thing, but sometimes it is a lot easier just to drop a name than it is to find a person. It is my business as the pastor, not only to get new members, but to keep up with the members I have. I am thinking now of a certain woman in the church where I now serve. That woman. (I sometimes wish she would join another church—she is a very disagreeable person!) One day she called me very upset over something in the church, and she said, "I am quitting the church." I got in my car and drove to her home. We sat together for an hour or so, and talked about the problem. I kept saying to her, "You cannot quit." I went back a second time and then I went back a third time, and eventually she came back. The pastor of the church must follow the example of the shepherd who went after that which is lost.

In my preaching I have sought to keep people in the church, but they also have a responsibility—in fact—two responsibilities. The first is to keep themselves from being lost. Years ago in the mountains of North Georgia, there was a little church that did not have a musical instrument. Some of the people were opposed to it, and even if they had had one, no one could have played it. But the younger generation came along and they wanted to buy one of those little reed organs for the church. They had a meeting of the congregation and discussed it, and finally took a vote. The group that wanted to buy the organ won out. When they did, Uncle Jim reached over, picked up his hat, stalked down the aisle, and out the door. They all thought they had lost Uncle Jim.

But the next preaching Sunday, here he came and took his accustomed seat. After the service someone said, "Uncle

Jim, we thought you had quit the church." With fire in his eyes he replied, "Do you think I would let a little organ stand between me and my Lord?"

But I know people in the church who let a lot less than an organ stand between them and their Lord. It's too easy for church members to get their feelings hurt and quit. They have a responsibility at this point.

In the second place, as I have said to the members of the church, it is their business to invite people and win people for the Lord into the church. The most effective means of evangelism is one person's inviting another person. It would be embarrassing (in most congregations) to ask the people to lift their hands if, during the past year, they have invited even one person to the church. We need to remember that a missionary is not necessarily one who crosses the sea, but a missionary is one who sees the cross.

16
About Judgment—Not Pleasant, But Real

ANOTHER WORD the minister is required to speak, if he is to speak all the words, is the word *judgment*. As I look back over my sermons, I must confess that this is a word that I have not spoken perhaps as much as I should have. It is not a pleasant word to speak, and some of the other words of life are much more pleasing. But I have preached about the judgment because I know it is real. Judgment is a word that measures the shallowness of our faith. It measures the limits of our devotion.

We need to be reminded that God is a God of judgment. Victor Hugo was asked if it would have been possible for

Napoleon to have won the battle of Waterloo. "No," he
answered. "Why? On account of Wellington, on account of
Blücher? No. On account of God. . . . The hour had come
for supreme, incorruptible justice to take notice. Napoleon
had been denounced in the infinite, and his downfall had
been determined; he was obstructing God."

Anne of Austria said to Richelieu: "My Lord Cardinal,
God does not pay at the end of every week, but at the end
He pays."

We can go on leaving God out, disobeying His laws, failing
in our duty to Him. But let us remember these words from
the Bible: "Be not deceived; God is not mocked: for whatso-
ever a man soweth, that shall he also reap" (Galatians 6:7).

We hear a lot about The Judgment Day, but every day is
Judgment Day. Whenever we face the light of the truth of
the love of God, we make a decision. Judgment continues
day after day; no act is ever complete in itself. When a thing
is done, it is not done with. Action is followed by reaction.
Day by day we gather the harvest of yesterday, and we are
sowing for the harvest of the future.

The judgments upon us, however, may go unnoticed until
a special moment. Some crisis or peril can reveal the coward-
ice that has been building up in a human soul. Some unex-
pected temptation may reveal a moral weakness that has
taken possession of our character. It has been said again and
again that what we do in an emergency is the result of what
we have been doing and thinking in the many uneventful
days which preceded.

The Bible truly teaches a final judgment of God. ". . .
Vengeance is mine; I will repay, saith the Lord" (Romans
12:19). We believe that God appears before us in judgment in
life and that we also appear before Him in judgment at death.
We read, ". . . for we shall all stand before the judgment seat

of Christ" (Romans 14:10). We wonder what happens five minutes after death.

However, as I preach about the judgment of God, I like to emphasize the fact that while we are judged by One who is firm and does not condone our faults, He is also faithful and does not forget our efforts. And as I pointed out elsewhere, at times I can say, "Thank God for Judgment Day." Not only is it a day when we are judged for our sins; it is also a time when the wrongs of life are righted.

17
About the Meanings of Grace

IN EVERY SERMON I have preached, I hope I have had a word about *grace*. The older I get, the more I am convinced of my need for grace. I can echo the words of Saint Paul when he said, "But by the grace of God, I am what I am . . ." (1 Corinthians 15:10). As we read the Bible, we find at least three distinct meanings for grace:

First, . . . *by grace ye are saved* (Ephesians 2:5). Grace here means the unmerited favor, the mercy, the loving-kindness of God. God has two hands—the hand of grace and the hand of judgment.

Grace is the ultimate expression of the love of God—the love that is seeking, selfless, suffering, saving, and supreme. As the shepherd searches for his lamb on the dark mountainside, so is God seeking man. Though His love was spit back into His face with the words, "He saved others; himself he cannot save . . ." (Matthew 27:42), His measureless love continues to climb new Calvarys, knowing that love through suffering will someday save from sin.

Grace might be described as the activity of God's love. As George Matheson expressed it, "O Love that wilt not let me go. . . ." Once at the moment of a very difficult decision, David Livingstone said, "I felt the downreach of the divine." Or, as we sometimes sing, "Though I forget Him and wander away,/Still He doth love me wherever I stray. . . ."

Someone has asked "Whence to the singer comes the song?" Nobody knows. A painter paints some object; a poem is an expression of intelligence, but music is a mystery. Out of the *everywhere* comes melody. Music was not invented; it was pressed upon man's soul.

Likewise—yet more mysterious than music—is our belief in God. Where did the idea of God come from? Certainly man did not just invent it. No man has ever proved God; he believes in God because he cannot do otherwise. The eye does not create light—rather does light create the eye. Destroy all light and soon the eyes will be destroyed. The fish in the dark rivers of Mammoth Cave are an illustration. Those fish cannot see because all their lives have been spent in darkness.

Likewise, man's belief in faith does not create the idea of God. Rather does the existence of God create the ability in man to believe and have faith. Just as one can become color-blind (which is the inability to properly interpret the light rays), or even become totally blind, so one can become God-blind. As we cut ourselves off from God by sin, we "wither away," as Jesus said of the branch, and become incapable of understanding or even feeling God at all.

By His grace God is ever seeking us. I had the privilege of preaching in a mission with Dr. Clarence E. Macartney. I remember a story that he told about a little girl in Scotland. She liked to go with her shepherd father and listen as he called the sheep. By and by when she grew to womanhood, she moved to the city away from the father, and eventually drifted into a life of wrong.

The word got back to her father and the old shepherd went to the city to find her. Day by day he walked the streets, but he never could see her. Then one day, he started walking down the middle of the street, sounding loud and clear the shepherd's call. This girl heard that voice—it was unmistakable. Her heart leaped within her; she rushed out into the street and into her father's arms.

This is the experience we sing about:

> Amazing grace! how sweet the sound—
> That saved a wretch like me!
> I once was lost, but now am found,
> Was blind but now I see.

Second, *grace means the strength and power of God.* Saint Paul tells how there was given to him "a thorn in the flesh." (*See* 2 Corinthians 12:7.) He prayed that it might depart from him. But that prayer was unanswered. Instead, he was given the grace to bear it. ". . . My grace is sufficient for thee . . ." (2 Corinthians 12:9).

The term "thorn in the flesh" sooner or later comes to have meaning for every person. For Milton it meant blindness; for Tennyson it meant loneliness; for Millet it was poverty; for each of us it means something. And, like Saint Paul, we pray repeatedly that our thorn might be removed. Often God does answer that prayer.

On the other hand, God often does something better than remove the thorn. He gives us the grace—the strength—to bear it. He gives us the power to overcome.

Here is an example: An oyster is quietly sleeping in the warmth of some sea. A tiny grain of sand is borne along on the current and is caught in the open shell of the oyster. An annoyance has entered into the oyster's life, but instead of fighting the intruder, the oyster proceeds to manufacture an exudation of gummy substance, which it spins around the "thorn in its flesh." Thus the thorn eventually becomes a pearl. Someone has said that "A pearl is a garment of patience which enclosed an annoyance."

There was Cardinal Mercier during World War I. His beautiful cathedral was bombed, his priceless books were destroyed, and some of his students were slain in cold blood. Out of that experience he wrote these words: "Suffering accepted and used will give you a serenity which may well prove the most exquisite fruit of your life."

Milton's blindness resulted in *Paradise Lost.* God's grace wrought *In Memoriam* out of Tennyson's loneliness—and "The Angelus" from Millet's poverty.

"We shroud the cages of birds," said Richter, "when we would teach them to sing."

God does not always save us from the storms, from the hurts, from the sorrows, and from all the unhappy experiences of life. Sometimes God saves us in the midst of those experiences. Out of those experiences—sometimes—comes the most beautiful pearl of our lives.

I hear people talk about how God sends suffering upon them. I really doubt that God ever puts the thorn in our flesh. The very circumstances of life do that. But in the very beginning, the thorn may become a blessing because it creates a sense of need. We drop our smugness; we are not as cocky. We begin to feel that we cannot handle life by ourselves. Eventually we reach the point of knowing that we are not sufficient unto ourselves. Anything that gives us a sense of the need of God is a blessing.

At this point, we cannot judge each other. Many times the

person we least suspect is carrying a burden that may be the heaviest. I had an experience about a year ago that brought this home to me more clearly. I was to preach in a large convention of the church. As I sat in the pulpit I saw in the congregation a certain bishop of the Methodist church. Now, I want to go on record right here as saying that I love all the bishops of the church. But, this particular one, I found the hardest to love. I had watched him through the years and I had felt that he was dictatorial. I had been critical of him. As I sat in the pulpit and saw him sitting out in the pew, I knew that he would be critical of me. I wished he were not there. But I went ahead and preached that sermon as best I could. After the benediction he lingered. Finally, he came up to me and said, "Charles, I would like to walk back to the hotel with you." As we walked along, he told me about a heavy burden that had been on his heart for many years. And he told me how that night my sermon had helped him more than anything he had ever heard. I realized I had been misjudging this man.

I have never seen suffering adequately explained. Time and again we have no answer for it. Jesus said, ". . . In the world ye shall have tribulation: but be of good cheer. . . ." What is the rest of that verse? Is it, "I have explained the world?" No. He says, ". . . I have overcome the world" (John 16:33). God's grace does not always explain nor remove the thorn, but it is always sufficient to overcome.

As the pastor of the church, I have cause every day to talk to people about the grace of God that can give them the strength they need in their hours of trial.

Third, *there is another meaning of grace in the Bible.* We remember that lovely scene when St. Paul was talking to the elders of the church at Ephesus. He was saying that soon he would be leaving them. He talked about his ministry among them, and after he had bid them good-bye, they knelt to-gether for prayer. Then we read, "And they all wept sore, and fell on Paul's neck, and kissed him" (Acts 20:37).

Ordinarily, the idea of men kissing other men can be even repulsive, but not in this instance. As I picture Paul in my mind, I see one who is rough in appearance, wearing cheap and ill-fitting clothes, frail and sickly, with stoop shoulders. He is not at all handsome. Yet, there is such a winsome attractiveness about him that he is actually magnetic. He is so lovable that it seems right and proper that even men should want to kiss him as they parted.

There is only one explanation. The same thing happened to Paul which happened to the first Christians. We read ". . . great grace was upon them all" (Acts 4:33). Here *grace* means *charm, beauty,* and *radiance.* It is a marvelous experi-ence for one to become graceful. It means they are poised, harmonious, free of conflict within themselves and with other people.

Some of my happiest experiences have been in the moun-tains. I remember particularly one evening when we were visiting at Lake Junaluska. Our three children were small and that evening we were going over to Cherokee, North Carolina. We fixed some sandwiches and drove to the top of the pass through the mountains, and stopped in a little park. There, late in the afternoon, we ate our sandwiches. It was a lovely evening; the air felt so clean; the sunshine on the distant peaks seemed more like halos. Food never tasted quite so good. We watched as the sun gradually dropped out of sight in reverent quietness. The very beauty of the world about us was refreshing. Even the children talked in subdued tones. The mountains, the trees, the little creek, even the rocks—they all seemed to cast a spell over us. I realized that "great grace was upon them all."

That was God's Creation, and God does the same thing for people. It is completely indescribable. How can you describe love? How can you describe sunlight? No person can give you a definition of beauty. There are some things you cannot hold in your hands. You cannot diagram them. Even the senses of hearing and seeing cannot completely take them in. There are some things you can feel only in your very soul.

It is a wonderful, beautiful thing when the grace of God descends on a person.

Grace—God's gracious mercy which gives us the assurance that our sins can be forgiven. *Grace*—the strength of God which makes us sufficient for all of our burdens. *Grace* —the charm, beauty, radiance of God, which descends upon a person.

The angel said to the apostles, ". . . speak in the temple to the people all the words of this life" (Acts 5:20). Now for forty-three years God has given me that privilege. He has given me opportunities I have never dreamed I would have. I have preached more sermons than there are days in those last forty-three years. I have preached at the Garden Tomb of Jesus, on a boat on the Sea of Galilee, on the Isle of Patmos, in Rome, in England, in Korea, and other places. It has been for me a thrilling, joyous experience.

As I mentioned before, God has given me the opportunity to preach through the columns of newspapers, as well as through my books. I wrote for the *Atlanta Journal* and the *Atlanta Constitution,* and now for the *Houston Chronicle* and a host of other papers. I am grateful for these opportunities.

I do not know how many more years I will have to preach. I hope many more, and I look forward to the future years with joyous anticipation. I think there has never been a more

exciting day in which to proclaim the glory of God than this
day in which we are now living.

I can say in the words of Charles Wesley:

> Happy, if with my latest breath
> I may but gasp His name;
> Preach Him to all, and cry in death,
> "Behold, behold the Lamb!"

IV
Principles I Have Lived By

18
Believing in People

As I LOOK BACK over the years of my ministry, I can discern certain principles that have been dominant in my thinking. I feel that these principles have pretty much shaped my life. The first one I would like to put down is this:

I believe in people.

My belief in people has come, mainly, I think, as a result of the people's belief in me. I have never served a church where I did not feel I had the enthusiastic support of the people of that church. I remember when I first went to the Grace Church in Atlanta. I remember the first Sunday. One of the men came to me and said, "Charles, I will be praying for you every day." That impressed me and I wrote that man's name down on a sheet of paper. From then on, every time somebody told me that he or she was praying for me, I would write that name down. Eventually I stopped the practice of writing the name down, but I had on my list of people who had told me that they were praying for me every day, a total of 1,837 names! That did a lot for me. Every time I walked into the pulpit, I knew that many people were praying for me.

This has been true in every church I ever served. I have never had any real opposition in the church. But, I have had countless people who have given to me their love, their support, and their prayers. It has just come naturally to me to believe in people, because I know so many have believed in me.

I need to go back to my first Sunday as a preacher. That Sunday shaped the course of my ministry. That was the most important day of my ministry. I shall never forget it as long as I live. It was in June of 1933 that I was appointed to Whitesburg, Georgia. I was only nineteen years old at the time. On Saturday I moved into the parsonage next door to the church. It was a large house with four bedrooms. The ladies had gone in and made up the beds with clean sheets in each of the four bedrooms. I was not married at that time, and I remember I started off sleeping in one room. When the sheets got dirty, I moved to the next room. Those four bedrooms lasted me the entire summer!

I never shall forget my first sermon. I had never preached before and, really, it was a frightening experience. Just about everybody in town came to hear the new preacher. And the church was full. I preached that morning on the Prodigal Son. I told the people everything I knew about the Prodigal Son, about his elder brother, and about his father. Then I told them everything else I knew about religion and about the church. When I finished that sermon I had exhausted my resources. I had preached a total of thirteen minutes.

As we sang the last hymn, I realized that I had been a failure that day. I further felt that preaching was not for me, and that I was going home that afternoon and they could get another preacher. I would have done it, too, except for one man. As long as I live, I shall never forget that man. He was Dr. George Washington Burnett. Dr. Burnett was more than eighty years old. He was a large man and a very impressive-looking man. He had long white hair; he looked like a prophet. He had been practicing medicine in that little town for more than fifty years. He was the biggest man in the church and in the community. He sat on the front seat that morning and I was really afraid of him. After the service I did not want to speak to him. I knew he would say something harsh to me about my poor preaching. After the benediction, he just sat in his pew until most of the other people had gone. Then he got up and walked over to me, and put his arm around me. I'll never forget his words. He said, "Charles, you helped me this morning. You are going home and eat dinner with me." I went home with the old doctor and his dear wife. During the dinner he talked about what a wonderful thing it is for a young man to enter the ministry, and how he can help so many people. He talked about how happy he was that I was a minister, and that he loved me, and wanted to help me. When I left Dr. Burnett's house that day, I had no idea of quitting.

I went to the School of Theology at Emory that Fall. Every Saturday I would go back out to Whitesburg and every Saturday night I would eat supper with Dr. Burnett and his wife. After supper, we would sit around the fire and he would ask me what I intended to preach about the next day. I would tell him my subject; then he would discuss it with me. I did not realize it at the time, but I later came to know that what he was doing was trying to give me something worthwhile to say in my sermon the next day. After every service, he would come up and put his arm around me, and he would always say the same thing: "Charles, you helped me this morning."

The next June, Leila and I got married. We married in her church which was named Trinity not far from her home in Clermont, Georgia. Just about an hour before time for our wedding, there came a telephone call from Whitesburg. The call told me that Dr. Burnett had died and they wanted me to come home and conduct his funeral service the next day. Leila and I had planned a little honeymoon. I never expected to take but one honeymoon and that meant a lot to both of us. Had it been anybody else in that church, I could have said get the pastor over in the next town. But not Dr. Burnett. I gave up the only honeymoon I ever expected to have. Love him—as long as there is a breath in my body, I will love that man. Why? He believed in me.

I have had a few people criticize me, but I don't really remember their names. They don't make any difference. The people that really make a difference are the people who believe in you.

One of the characters of the Bible that I have appreciated and loved the most is a man named Barnabas. I have preached at least a hundred times on Barnabas. Let me tell you how I got interested and came to know him. My father was in the hospital. He had cancer and he knew that he was not going to live. During those weeks before he died, I had the privilege of spending a lot of time with him. I never shall forget one night that he told me that when he died he would like to have a marker put at his grave. On that marker he would like to have his name, the date of his birth, and the date of his death. Then he said that if those who know him the best could say it sincerely, he would like to have on his marker HE WAS A GOOD MAN.

That really disappointed me. I would like to have said something stronger and better than that about my father. Just to say that somebody is good is not very exciting. I have always felt that one of the worst remarks anybody can make is, "He can't preach, but he's a good man." Nobody considers that a compliment.

After my father died, I looked up that expression in the Bible. I found it in Acts 11:24. Here being discussed is Barnabas, and the Bible says, "For he was good a man, and full of the Holy Ghost and of faith. . . ." I read everything in the Bible on Barnabas and I got acquainted with him. He was a man who had faith in God, but he was especially noted for his faith in his fellowman.

Saul of Tarsus was one of the persecutors of the early church. One day he came to the Christians and told them that he had been converted, and that now his name was Paul. He wanted to join with them and preach the Gospel of Christ. Those first Christians did not trust him, and they would not accept him. Then it was that Barnabas said, in effect, "Paul, I believe in you. You can work with me." They went out together. The greatest Christian preacher the world has ever known was saved for the kingdom and saved for the church because somebody believed in him.

Later, a bright young man joined Barnabas and Paul. His name was John Mark. After a time, Mark got homesick. He quit and went back. He was young and tender. After a time he came back and wanted to go with them again. Then we read, "But Paul thought it not good to take him with them." (*See* Acts 15:38.) Paul was hard and tough. He had no place for a quitter.

Barnabas said something like this, "Paul, I would rather be with you than anybody. But I believe this boy, John Mark, still can be valuable in the kingdom. I am not willing to let him go." Even though it meant separation from his best friend, Barnabas was willing to give Mark another chance. So we read, "Barnabas took Mark, and sailed unto Cyprus"

(v. 39). Later on the first person to write the story of our Lord's life was this young man, John Mark. He was saved for the church, saved for the kingdom, because somebody believed in him.

As we read the four Gospels, we hear our Lord saying some very harsh things to certain people. Some people He called *hypocrites*. Others He called *vipers*. But according to the record, even Jesus never won a person that He criticized.

Across the years of my ministry, I have never felt it was my duty to fuss at people or criticize them. I have never felt that it was necessary to preach much about their sins. Most people know about their sins. I have felt it was my job to let people know that the preacher was concerned about them and loved them, and believed in them, and wanted to help them. This has been a controlling principle of my life.

While I was pastor at Blue Ridge, Georgia, I was the Boy Scoutmaster. In the troop was a big, overgrown boy, who really grew up without much of a chance. He was considered one of the bad boys of the community. In school and in the town, he was constantly blamed for things that went wrong. He had a reputation of being tough and hard. I never shall forget once something happened and some of the boys were blaming this particular boy. He listened to their accusations —fully expecting some form of punishment—but without flinching. Finally, I said, "Now, let's hear his side." He started to cry. I was surprised and all the other boys were surprised. Nobody had ever seen this boy cry before. I asked what was the matter. I can hear him now, as if it were yesterday. He said, "Nobody ever said before that I had a side."

In our judgments of other people, I have always felt we ought to wait until we hear their side. Everybody has a side.

19
Living Affirmatively

I FEEL AS IF—for the most part—I have lived affirmatively. That is, I have tried to concentrate on possibilities instead of problems. I believe it is better to emphasize our triumphs than our troubles. I believe there is more power in thinking about our Saviour than about our sins. There is more power in emphasizing our faith instead of our fears.

One of the things I have always believed in is healing through prayer. I have spent a great deal of time praying for people who were sick. But many times we do ourselves more harm than good with our praying. I can just picture some person praying, "Lord, I am sick. Lord, You just do not realize how sick I am. Feel my forehead, Lord; what a temperature I have! My back hurts; my stomach is all upset. Lord, I feel so bad I want You to heal me." That kind of prayer never heals anybody. It makes them sicker; it makes me sort of sick even talking about it.

Once I was driving along the highway and the traffic was stopped. On the side of the road I saw some men sinking some large steel beams into the ground. I asked one of the men what he was doing. He explained to me that the ground under the road was shifting. They were sinking some of these beams to give stability to the roadbed.

I have always felt that it was of great value to sink into one's mind some great truths. Suppose one really comes to understand and accept this truth:

The Lord is my shepherd; I shall not want.

Just that one statement can tremendously affect a life.

We come to moments of sorrow, of disappointment, of hurt. We have these periods of depression and defeat. But during those times, if deep in our minds are some of the great positive truths of God, they give us strength and stability and keep us going.

One of the problems that I have had across the years of my ministry is with certain people who emphasize the negatives. It is an easy thing to make a list of what you do not do—like: smoking, dancing, playing cards, drinking alcohol, and so on. But no amount of *don'ts* add up to a Christian. The Christian life is determined more by what we do do than what we do not do. In my preaching, I have never been much of a *don't* preacher. We need more *do* preaching.

Across the years, I have enjoyed George Bernard Shaw. I guess he would not be classified as one of the greatest Christians who ever lived, but he is one of the most penetrating thinkers I have ever read. One of his plays is entitled *Too True to Be Good.* In the third act a character by the name of Aubrey says this:

> . . . Is no enough? For a boy, yes; for a man, never. Are we any the less obsessed with a belief when we are denying it than when we were affirming it? No: I must have affirmations to preach. Without them the young will not listen to me; for even the young grow tired of denials. The negative-monger falls before the soldiers, the men of action, the fighters, strong in the old uncompromising affirmations which give them status, duties, certainty of consequences; so that the pugnacious spirit of man in them can reach out and strike death-blows with steadfastly closed minds. Their

way is straight and sure; but it is the way of death; and the preacher must preach the way of life. . . .

George Bernard Shaw
Too True to Be Good
Act III

20
Making Decisions in God's Presence

EVERY LIFE is determined by decisions. Sometimes it is very frightening to me as I look back and see how the seemingly very small decisions determined my entire life—and even affected the lives of other people. The older I grow, and the more of life I have seen, the more I have felt the need of God's strength and guidance in making decisions.

For example, some years ago, I was given the choice of moving to one of two churches. I would have been delighted to have been the pastor of either of the churches. As far as I could see, the benefits and the opportunities were about the same in each church. One Tuesday morning I went to my study, but somehow I could not get my mind on my work. I sat there all the morning thinking and praying. I am sure I must have spent an hour on my knees that morning. I was asking God's guidance in making that decision, but somehow no answer seemed to come. That afternoon I also played golf, but I played one of the poorest games I ever played. My mind was just not on it. About nine o'clock that night the phone rang. Calling was a bishop from another state. He said he would like to talk to me later in the week about coming to the church in his area. Suddenly everything was clear to me. I said, "Bishop, appoint me right at this moment and I will come." His reply was, "You are appointed."

I have thought of that decision many times. It not only affected my life, but it affected the lives of my children. Who they married was determined by that decision. If I had gone to the other city, they would have married other people. We have eight grandchildren. If I had gone to the other city, we would not have any of those eight grandchildren. Hopefully, we would have some other grandchildren, but they would not be the same ones. And I could go on talking about the effects of that decision. I have felt across these years that somehow, as I prayed that day, God put the answer in my mind and when the time came, I knew exactly what to do and what to say. As I look back, I believe it was the right decision. I emphasize that if we make our decisions in God's presence, we have wisdom and insight that we would not have otherwise.

Across the years, I have spent many hours in personal counseling. And I do not mind saying that in this field I have now become an expert. I think I am one of the best counselors in the United States. (I am modest about it, but I also want to be honest.) I used to think people coming to me wanted my advice about things. But now I have learned better. To be an expert counselor, really all that is required is to ask two questions and be quiet. I have done it hundreds and hundreds of times. For example, not long ago, a man came in to see me saying that he had a very serious problem. He was so nervous he could hardly talk. When he sat down, he sat on the edge of the chair. He acted as if he thought the chair might fall under him just any moment. I told him that was a good sturdy chair and that he should just sit back and relax. And I told him this story:

When I started in the ministry, I had a very serious problem. Every time I preached my throat became so hoarse that I could hardly speak. Numerous times I went to other churches to preach three or four nights, and after the second night I would have to come home. I went to doctors but nobody could help me. As long as I live I'll never forget one night. I was preaching in the First United Methodist Church of Austell, Georgia. The pastor of that church was Reverend J. T. Robbins. I will never forget that man. After the service, he waited until everybody was gone. Then he had me sit down and he said to me that I was going to ruin my throat. I told him that I knew that, but I didn't know anything to do about it. His reply was, "I am going to tell you what to do about it."

He explained to me that I was too tense when I was preaching and that I should learn to relax. He said that this tension not only went over my body, but particularly to my vocal chords. He insisted that it would not be much longer until my ability to speak would be destroyed. That meant I would have to give up the ministry and it was a frightening thought for me.

He went on to explain that when I preached he had noticed that I kept my hands tightly clinched all the time. Then he gave me the wisest advice anybody has ever given me. He said, "Charles, remember when you preach always keep your hands relaxed." It has now been nearly forty years since that night, but from then until now, I have never had throat trouble anymore. I may not be the best preacher you ever heard, but I have the most relaxed hands you have ever seen!

Across the years, I have had a lot of fun with this. I fly in airplanes a great deal. Nearly every person in an airplane is a little nervous, especially when we get into some turbulence. I watch people sitting in the seat beside me and—almost invariably—during turbulence people will take hold of the arms of their seats and hold as tightly as they can. Over and over, I have asked people why they are holding on to those seats, and I have explained that the seat belt will hold them, and there is no way they could get out of the seat no matter how turbulent the air is. I suggest that they turn loose the arm rest, and begin to relax their hands. Really, it is miraculous how a person begins to lose tension and settle down when their hands become relaxed.

Between my wife and me, this has been a happy experience. Every so often, when one or the other of us would get a little irritated, the other would say, "Now before you say anything, relax your hands." It is amazing how relaxed hands will soften your comment.

There was an old lady not long ago out in West Texas who said to me, "I have learned how to sit loose."

Anyway, back to my story: I got this man who had come to see me for counseling relaxed. Then I asked him my first question, "What is your situation?" I sat quietly and carefully listened to every word that he said. He told me his entire story.

When he finished, then I asked my second question, "What do you think you ought to do about it?" Again, I sat and listened as he gave me his answer. When he finished I said, "I think you have it right there. That is what I would do."

He got up; he took my hand; he said to me, "You have solved my problem."

Now, I say that is good counseling. The truth is, I did help him. He did not need me to tell him what to do. Most of the time, we are not confused. Most of the time we know the answers. We just do not want to do what we know we ought to do. But sitting there in the church, with the minister, this man felt a support that enabled him to make his decision.

Go back and read the thrilling story of Moses and the burning bush. You will find it in the third chapter of the Book of Exodus. Moses was out there watching over the sheep. I daresay that every day he would think about how that he ought to go back and face up to Pharaoh and demand freedom for his people, but Moses could not make the decision to go back. He did not have the nerve or the willpower, or he did not believe he had the strength. Then one day he saw a bush on fire. The bush kept burning, but it was not consumed. He went over to the bush and he realized that God was present. He was so impressed in the presence of God, that he even pulled off his shoes. He was standing on holy ground. There in God's presence, Moses made the decision to go back and face Pharaoh.

Read the story of our Lord in Gethsemane, which is recorded in the twenty-second chapter of Saint Luke's Gospel. We remember how that He prayed with His disciples that night. After a while He got up and went a little farther with Peter and James and John. They were his three closest friends. There are some decisions that any person can help us make—just anyone we might meet on the street can render aid in some decisions. But there are some decisions only certain people that we love and trust the most can help us make.

But then we read, that Jesus went a little farther. There are some decisions that can only be made alone with God. Then it was that He prayed, ". . . nevertheless, not my will, but thine, be done" (v. 42).

There is great power when we make our decisions in His presence. This is one of the principles that I have believed in for a long, long time, and I have sought to practice it. There have been times when I hurriedly made a decision before I prayed. And there have been times when I regretted it. But when I really feel I am in God's presence, somehow, the right decision has always seemed easy for me.

I have loved James Russell Lowell's hymn:

Once to every man and nation comes the moment
    to decide;
In the strife of Truth with Falsehood, for the good
    or evil side;
Some great cause, God's new Messiah, offering each
    the bloom or blight,
And the choice goes by forever 'twixt that darkness
    and that light.

It is frightening sometimes to realize how that one's entire life can be changed by just one decision. Decisions have a way of not waiting and if we evade and compromise, decisions move on out of our reach and we are left behind in defeat. No one has ever put it better than Shakespeare:

There is a tide in the affairs of men,
Which, taken at the flood, leads on to fortune;
Omitted, all the voyage of their life
Is bound in shallows and in miseries.
                        Julius Caesar, Act IV, scene 3

21
Having the Power of Faith

INCREASINGLY through the years I have believed that no person is ever defeated until he or she thinks he is. We have tremendous powers if we use them. One of the ministers in my early years that I loved and gained a lot from was Dean Ramundo de Ovies. He was dean of the Episcopal Cathedral in Atlanta, Georgia, for many years. I had the privilege of being with him on a number of occasions and he always inspired me. He was a great storyteller and I never shall forget one story that he told me. Really, I have heard this story credited to other sources, but nobody ever told it better than Dean de Ovies, and I am happy to give him full credit for it.

When he was a boy he lived in England. He explained that they had a habit of catching sparrows in the cemeteries at night. The next day their mother would make sparrow pie and it was delicious. He explained to me that it would usually take about twenty sparrows to make a pie. These sparrows would roost in the vines of the cemetery and while they were asleep, they were easily caught.

One night he was in the cemetery catching sparrows and he fell into a newly dug grave. The grave was so deep that he could not get out. He tried every way he knew but would fail. Finally, in exhaustion, he sat down in a corner to wait until morning. Presently he heard the footsteps of another boy, who had come into the graveyard looking for sparrows. The boy was whistling—as people are apt to do in graveyards at night. He recognized him as his friend, Charlie. His first thought was to call out to Charlie and ask his help, but he decided to wait for a while and see what happened. Sure enough, Charlie slipped into the same grave. Dean de Ovies explained that he sat quietly in the corner as Charlie tried to get out. But, neither could he climb over the side. After a while, Dean de Ovies said in a deep voice, "Can't you let a man enjoy his own grave in peace?"

The result was electric. Charlie got out over the side of that grave as if he had wings. He thought he could not get out of that grave, but he discovered that he could!

As I say, I have seen that story attributed to other sources, but no matter—it illustrates what I am trying to say. I believe we all have unused powers with which, if properly motivated, we can accomplish things we never dreamed we could accomplish.

In my book *Prayer Changes Things* I have three chapters on the power of faith. But here let me sum up very quickly and briefly what I tried to say in those three chapters. There are five laws of faith:

First, *you have faith.* Ever so often somebody will ask the question, "How can I find faith?" Or, I hear people say, "I have lost my faith." Life has a way of smothering our faith. Loved ones can die, businesses can fail, jobs can be lost, friends can betray, lives can be ruined. Wrecks and fires and earthquakes and wars, and all the troubles of life can come in upon us. They have a tendency to fill our minds and overwhelm us. But the truth is, no person ever loses faith.

I love the old Chinese tale—the source of which I do not know—of the fish who overheard the fisherman say, "Have you ever stopped to think how essential water is? Without water the world would dry up and all life would die."

The little fish in the lake, when they heard that, became panic-stricken. They began saying to each other, "We must hurriedly find water at once." They asked the other fish in the lake where to find water, but no one seemed to know. Finally, they swam out into the river, but the fish in the river could not tell them where to find water. Finally, they swam into the deepest part of the ocean. There they found an old fish and they asked him where to find water. He replied, "You are in water right now—you have never left it."

So it is with our faith. We are born with it; we never really lose it.

Second, *always start with your faith instead of your fears.* I knew a lady who was paralyzed in one leg. She was spending all of her time in a rolling chair. Her doctor said to her that she ought to get up and walk. But she protested that because of her paralyzed leg, she could not possibly walk.

The doctor had her stand up and then told her to walk. She put forth this paralyzed leg and as she moved her weight on to it she immediately began to fall. He caught her. Then he said to her, "Remember, you can always walk if you will step out on your good leg first."

Third, *no matter what happens, hold on to your faith.* In Vienna, Austria, it has long been sport to swim down the Danube River. But in the river there are whirlpools and sometimes a swimmer will get caught in a whirlpool and will drown. Wise swimmers know that when one is caught in a whirlpool, if one will just be still, the whirlpool will push the swimmer back to the surface and to safety.

In the stream of life we get caught in troubles and sometimes we get panicky, but if we will just keep our cool, gradually we will rise above this problem.

Fourth, *do not be afraid to trust your heart.* It was Pascal who said, "The heart has its reasons which reason knows nothing of."

Faith is never unreasonable, but sometimes we have deep impulses that we cannot explain. Sometimes our feelings are stronger than our reasons, and many times we ought to obey our deep feelings.

Fifth, *maintain a spirit of humility.*

I have long remembered the story of the college girl who visited the home of Beethoven. She slipped under the rope and began playing Beethoven's piano. She said to the one in charge, "I suppose every musician who comes here wants to play this piano?"

He explained to her that recently the great Paderewski was visiting there and someone asked him to play that piano. He replied, "No, I do not feel worthy to play the great master's piano." That story has always made a profound impression upon me.

I know that at times I have been accused of being less than

humble—perhaps at times justly so—but really I do not think so. I have spent my life in places and in positions that I did not feel worthy of. The first time I ever stood up to preach, I did not feel worthy to stand in that pulpit, and I was very uncomfortable. Really, that has been my experience through the years. I have always felt a genuine inadequacy for every job that I have had. Especially have I felt misjudged by my preacher friends. If they knew the actual truth, I believe they would say, "Charles knows the meaning of humility."

I think many, many times of that night in Gethsemane when the disciples did not feel the need to pray. I have always felt that need.

22
Knowing Your Deepest Desire

GEORGIA HARKNESS used to say, "Be careful what you set your heart on, for you will surely get it."

My wife is fond of telling about the first date we ever had. We were students at Young Harris College in North Georgia. And in those years, the rules were very strict in reference to the boys and the girls. They would let us have a date for two hours on Sunday afternoon. She tells how we sat out on a bench on the campus and talked during those two hours. The truth of the matter is they watched us so closely, all you could do *was* talk. Anyway, she says that I spent those two hours telling her that some day I was going to be the pastor of a large church in a big city. I was sixteen years old at the time. I had never lived in a city, and I knew nothing about large churches, but I knew what I wanted.

Now I can say that I got the church and I also got the girl.

I think the trouble with a lot of people is they never know what they want. Across the years, I have used a six-part formula that has really worked for me. Let me share it with you:

First, *decide what you really want.* Many people go through life never getting anywhere because they never know where they want to go. They never hit anything, because they never aim at anything. God gave to us a marvelous mechanism called "imagination." Just as a motion picture projector can flash on a screen a picture, so can we put on the screen of our minds a picture of whatever we want to put there. Decide what you want and flash it on the screen of your mind. Take it off; put it back; take it off; put it back. Keep doing that until that picture becomes clear and sharp and then keep it there.

Second, *write down on paper this dominant desire of yours.* When you first write it down, it may take a page, or even two or three pages. But then set to work to condense the idea. Keep working until you can state your deepest desire clearly in not more than fifty words. It is amazing how much one can say in fifty words if one really works at it. Reduce what you want to fifty or less written words.

Third, *after you have stated this idea in not more than fifty words, then memorize it and several times each day repeat it aloud.* I have found it to be helpful to repeat my desires looking into a mirror. At first one feels a bit foolish doing this, but it really is effective.

When once my mind becomes firmly set on an idea, obstacles begin to get out of the way as that idea moves forward.

Fourth, *test your idea.* Is it good for you? Is it fair to all other people concerned? Are you ready for it now? Do you honestly feel it is according to the will of God? Underneath all of this thinking is the insistence that one must rid one's life of selfishness. When we think only of ourselves, live only for ourselves, are concerned only for own good, then we have destroyed the very reason for living. No person really begins to live until he or she begins to live for God and for others. We must always remember the words of our Lord, "He that findeth his life shall lose it: and he that loseth his life for my sake shall find it" (Matthew 10:39).

Fifth, *after clarifying your thinking, and thoroughly testing your motives and purposes, then you are ready for the main thing—begin to pray.* I cannot count the times that I have turned to the eleventh chapter of Mark and read:

> And Jesus answering saith unto them, Have faith in God. For verily I say unto you, That whosoever shall say unto this mountain, Be thou removed, and be thou cast into the sea; and shall not doubt in his heart, but shall believe that those things which he saith shall come to pass; he shall have whatsoever he saith. Therefore, I say unto you, What things soever ye desire, when ye pray, believe that ye receive them, and ye shall have them.
>
> Verses 22–24

It is amazing what the reading of that passage will do for a person who is about to pray. I have watched baseball pitchers warm up before a game, but I think it is far more important to warm up before you begin to pray. That passage warms me up and conditions my mind.

It begins by telling me to have faith in God. Many things may be impossible in my own strength—but nothing is impossible with God. That passage talks about moving mountains. Too often I have concentrated on my problems instead of my powers.

Sixth—and don't leave this one out—*do all you can to accomplish your own desire.* Many times—in fact I would say, most times—instead of answering my prayers, God gives me the power and the opportunity to answer my own prayers.

But I go back to the place where I started: *Decide what you want.* One of the most dramatic scenes in all of Shakespeare is in *Hamlet.* You remember the occasion when the king went into the church to pray. He worked at it for a while, but his prayers did not reach the ceiling. I have had that same feeling. I have felt there were times when I just made no contact when I prayed. After a while, the king gave it up and went outside the chapel. There he explained the reason for his failure in prayer in the chapel. I think this is one of the best things Shakespeare ever wrote. He said:

> My words fly up, my thoughts remain below:
> Words without thoughts never to heaven go.
> *Hamlet,* Act III, scene 3

The Bible says the very same thing: "Let the words of my mouth, and the meditation of my heart, be acceptable in thy sight, O LORD, my strength, and my redeemer" (Psalms 19:14).

Many times we say words that we do not mean. We are not fooling God. Know what you want. But I must not leave this section without a brief mention of two very important additional principles. One is, we will have disappointments and it might be, as someone else has put it, "My disappointment may be God's appointment." If you fail in what you want, it may be that God has something better for you.

One of the cities that I have enjoyed visiting is Edinburgh, Scotland. I have walked several times down to the very impressive monument to Sir Walter Scott. Robert Louis Stevenson called him the "king of romantics." In his day Scott was the most popular writer. His works will be read as long as the world stands. I shall never forget reading his novels such as *Waverley, Ivanhoe, Kenilworth, Rob Roy,* and others. But Scott did not want to be a novelist; he wanted to be a poet. As a poet he failed. He was so ashamed of his first novels that he published them anonymously. But, he achieved greatness out of a disappointment.

I think of Whistler the artist. When the United States wanted to issue a stamp in honor of mothers, his picture of his mother was chosen. Whistler did not want to be an artist. He wanted to be a soldier. He went to West Point, but he flunked out. As a last resort, he took up painting.

Many times the thing we think we want, may not really be the thing that God wants for us.

A second thing that I want to emphasize very briefly is the fact that God will always give us another chance. The first sermon I preached was on the Prodigal Son. The father welcomed the boy back home. I have sought to emphasize this all during my ministry: If you have failed, God will still let you come back and try again.

When I lived in Atlanta, Georgia, one of the men that I appreciated the most was Ernest Rogers. He wrote a column for the *Atlanta Journal,* which was very popular, and he was a very beloved person of that city. Ernest and I became good friends, and we talked together about many things. There was a chapter in his life of which he was not proud. In fact, he went about to the depths of living. But he came back and, until his death, was a respected man.

One day he gave me a copy of a poem that he had written. I do not believe it has ever been published, but he told me if I ever wanted to use it, I would be welcome to do so. I want

to publish it now. I have read it many times, and it has given
me inspiration. All of us know failure, but all of us need to
be told that we can start over again. Read what Ernest
Rogers wrote. It is entitled "Another Chance" and it goes
like this:

> Maybe I failed in the final drive,
>   When sinew and nerve and heart
> Had lost the urge and the will to strive—
>   And I played the loser's part.
>
> But down on my trembling knees I fall,
>   Though others may look askance—
> To say a prayer to the Lord of All—
>   The God of another chance.
>
> Those who have drunk from the bitter cup,
>   And tasted the dregs of defeat—
> May win again, if lifted up
>   And placed in the mercy seat.
>
> Lord, I search through the darkling skies
>   For a word or a sign or a glance—
> That brings new light to my dimming eyes,
>   From the God of another chance.
>
> "Winner take all" is the way of the pack,
>   The losers must weep alone;
> The way is hard if they struggle back
>   To try it again on their own.
>
> But there is hope for the winner's share,
>   For those who would advance—
> By lifting up abiding prayer
>   To the God of another chance.

So down on my trembling knees I fall,
    Though others may look askance—
To say a prayer to the Lord of All—
    The God of another chance.

23
Taking Time for God

BROTHER LAWRENCE said it the best: "Practice the presence of God." A long time ago I decided that probably the worst sin of my own life was being in too big of a hurry. I made some changes and for many years I have not been in a hurry. I have learned that I have time to do whatever I want to do. One of the traps that preachers fall into is saying, "I am too busy." One reason we fall into this trap is because so many people say it to us. I could not count the times somebody has said to me, "I know how busy you are." Read the New Testament and you do not find one instance when Jesus was ever in a hurry. There is no record that Jesus ever ran anywhere!

As He walked through a crowd of people, a woman touched the hem of His garment and He stopped. A blind man cried out to Him from the side of the road and He turned aside to minister to that man. The truth is, there is no instance where Jesus was ever too busy when somebody needed His help.

If I were to name what I consider to be the worst sin in America it would be the sin of being too busy. We are in too big of a hurry; we are all the time rushing. I have a story that illustrates my point, and one that I always enjoy telling.

Some American explorers went to a certain remote section

of Africa to explore an area. They obtained some native guides. The first morning they got up early and they rushed all day. The second morning they got up early and they rushed all day. The third morning they got up early and they rushed all day. That is typical of Americans—always rushing somewhere.

One morning these American explorers got up to go rushing and the native guides were sitting out under a tree. The American explorers said, "Come on; we are in a hurry." The guides replied, "We no go today. We rest today to let our souls catch up with our bodies." The thought occurs to me that we are sending missionaries to them. I sometimes wonder who ought to be sending missionaries where!

During World War II, some American boys visited a volcano. One of the boys looked down at that boiling mass of lava and said, "It looks like hell." The native guide replied, "I declare, you Americans have been everywhere."

Not long ago, I visited one of the most prominent men in my city. He had been in an automobile wreck and was required to lie flat on his back for three weeks. I sat by his bedside one day and talked to him for a good while. I pointed out that he was very successful, he was highly respected in the community, he made a lot of money, and everybody thought well of him. But, I also pointed out that I did not see him at church as often as I used to. I also asked him if he had as much time to be with his two teenage boys as he once had. We talked along those lines for a time, and then I said to him, "Bill, while you are on your back, this is a good time for you to look up."

I have heard preachers say, "God puts us on our backs in order to give us a chance to look up." I have problems with the theology of that statement. I question that God caused my friend to have an automobile wreck, and I question that

God does a lot of things that cause people to be on their backs. But life has a way of putting us on our backs, and when we are on our backs, it's a good time to look up. The truth is, we ought to spend some time every day looking up without being forced to.

A long time ago, I decided that God gave some people more money than I will ever have. He also gave some people more talents and abilities than I will ever have. He also gave some people more opportunities than I will ever have. But God gave to me the same amount of time that He gave anybody else. I have twenty-four hours in every day. Nobody has any more hours than I have, and I decided that I would spend some of my own time. I am a bit like a friend of mine who once said to me, "I have never been happier since I resigned as General Manager of the Universe." I long ago learned that I did not have to do everything.

In the church where I am now the pastor, we conduct an average of four funerals a week. We have an average of four weddings a week. In addition, we will have normally about three hundred hospital calls to make every week. I could not begin to count the number of calls we have for counseling and all types of services. But I realize that I do not have to do all of these other things. There are five other ministers associated with me. I have never used the term *associate* pastors. We are all ministers together and I know that other ministers on my staff conduct a funeral or wedding or make a hospital visit just as well as I can. I have learned that I do not have to do everything. I do what I can do and I do not worry about the rest.

This has come very hard for me, because one of my greatest problems has been impatience. I wanted to get everything done today, and if it was not done I would get very discouraged. I know what it is to have dreams and hopes and be defeated, and then I would become very unhappy. But, many years ago, I read a book entitled *The Town With the Funny Name*. It was written by Max Miller. Out of that book, I copied a passage which I have read many, many times. It has been a great blessing to me and let me share it with you:

> When the heavier fogs come in along this immediate coast, we usually can see these fogs five or six miles ahead of time. For such a fog forms like a wall out there, and nothing is between us and the moving wall to intercept the vision. There are no trees or buildings out there, but only the surface of the sea, and across this surface the fog bank glides directly at us coming ever closer and more smoothly to submerge us finally.
>
> Part of the sky still will be baby blue, even directly above the fog bank. But when ultimately the fog bank, a muffled juggernaut, finally reaches us and overruns us there will be no blue anywhere, and no sky, and even our own hands may assume a strange pallor, and the only noticeable sound will be the distant foghorn on the lighthouse at the base of Point Loma.
>
> How many times now, I wonder, have we watched the wall of fog come in like this, and have known ahead of time just what it would do, how it would blind us, and yet know there is no answer for our blindness except to wait. And our most depressive days can be like this too, days which have no vision and no answer, and when only the experience of many years has taught us that such days will go away again. They will dissolve quite on their own and go away.

I have now learned that time can be my best friend. Rarely a night passes that I do not receive several telephone calls between midnight and two o'clock. I do not object to these calls. I have learned to go back to sleep quickly, but I have also learned that the person calling needs help at that very moment. Usually it is a person who lives alone. This person has some problem, and problems are worse at night than they are in the daytime. The person goes to bed, but cannot go to sleep and gradually gets more worried and worried. Frequently, this is a person who has been listening to me over the radio or the television, and my name comes to mind. Most of the time it is somebody I do not know. I talk patiently with this person and often I say that there is nothing he or she can do about this problem tonight. My suggestion is that we lay the problem aside now, and go to sleep, and then tomorrow call me again, and let's talk some more.

I cannot count the times that people have called me back the next day and said, "Things are a lot better now."

In his *Ring and the Book* Browning uses that wonderful line "I knew a necessary change in things." Our moments of defeat and sorrow are hard to bear, but we do bear those moments because we are certain of a "necessary change in things." In the Bible is the phrase *it came to pass*. One of my favorite sermons is on that phrase. There are a lot things in life that will pass if we give them time.

Since impatience has been a problem of mine, I think I have particularly noted certain verses in the Bible and committed to memory. Verses such as: "Wait on the LORD: be of good courage, and he shall strengthen thy heart: wait, I say, on the LORD" (Psalms 27:14). Another one that has meant so much to me is: "Why art thou cast down, O my soul? . . . hope thou in God . . ." (Psalms 42:11). Still another is "Rest in the LORD, and wait patiently for him . . ." (Psalms 37:7).

One of my favorite verses is this one: "For his anger endureth but a moment; in his favour is life: weeping may endure for a night, but joy cometh in the morning" (Psalms 30:5).

The thing I am trying to say is, that I have decided that I do not have to run through life. I am just not in as big a hurry as I used to think I had to be, and the amazing thing is I feel like I accomplish a lot more now than I used to!

There is a little phrase that has been in my mind for some years. It goes like this:

The hurrier I am, the behinder I get.

Before I leave this point there is one other phrase I would like to quote which I have remembered a long time. It goes like this: "He who cannot let go—cannot hang on."

24
Letting God Control Me

MANY TIMES we think of religion as some sort of magic power. We think of prayer as a means of accomplishing what we want. But really, the Christian faith is putting my life in God's hands. Prayer is committing my will to God's will. As I grow in my faith, I realize that the important thing is not my controlling God, but rather God's controlling me.

In Houston is one of the greatest medical centers in the world. I happen to serve on the board of one of the hospitals, and I visit there a great deal. Not long ago, one of the doctors was showing me a new X-ray machine which had been purchased. It is one of the most powerful X-ray machines obtainable. He told me a great deal about what they can now do with that type of therapy. I asked him what X-ray is. I knew he could not answer that question, but I wanted to hear what he would say. He replied that he did not know what

X-ray is, and neither did anyone else know. But we have
learned to build a machine, and through that machine we run
a power called electricity. Nobody knows what electricity is.
But out of that machine comes X-ray, and marvelous and
wonderful things can be developed.

I believe that a person is a much more wonderful mechanism than an X-ray machine is, and the power of God is a
much greater power than electricity is. I believe that when
God's power begins to flow through a human life—even my
own life—that wonderful and marvelous things can be accomplished.

We used to sing a little gospel song which said, "Nothing
between my soul and the Saviour." Through the years of my
ministry, I have felt increasingly that it be the desire of my
heart and life that there be nothing between God and me. I
like the phrase that Dr. Frank Laubach used to use: *clear
channels.* It is wonderful what God can do with a person
who is a clear channel. I have seen, even in my own ministry,
things happen that could not be explained apart from the
power of God. I have no power. I have no ability to help
anybody, but I believe God working through me can have
power and can work miracles.

I have a story that has meant very much to me. It is not
new. (The truth is that nearly every preacher has told this
story.) But it is still a good story, and it is worth hearing.

Once a very famous violinist was to give a concert in a
certain city. He owned one of the finest Stradivarius violins
in existence. For several days the newspapers in this city
wrote stories about this man's coming concert. Each of the
stories featured this very rare and valuable violin. The morning of the concert, there was a picture of the violin on the
front page of the paper.

That night the concert hall was crowded. The violinist

walked on the stage and played his first number. It was beautifully done, and when he finished, the entire audience stood and gave him thunderous applause.

Then he walked over to a chair and smashed his violin across the back of that chair into a thousand pieces. There was a gasp from the audience.

Then he turned to the microphone and said to the people that he had read the stories about his concert and how that his violin had been featured. He noted that instead of his picture on the front page of the paper, they had put the picture of his violin. He explained that that afternoon he had walked up the street to a cheap pawnshop. There he purchased a violin for five dollars. He put some strings on it. Then he said, "I know it disturbed you to see me smash this violin, but I wanted you to know that the violinist is more important than the violin."

I have thought of that story all through my ministry. I realize I do not have great talent. I may not be any more than a cheap pawnshop violin, but I also know that if I am in God's hands that He can use me—even me—in His service. This has been for me a source of great encouragement and strength.